READING
to your baby

Techniques that bring language alive for your little ones

ALISON L R DAVIES

CARROLL & BROWN PUBLISHERS LIMITED

First published in 2010 in the United Kingdom by

Carroll & Brown Publishers Limited
20 Lonsdale Road
London NW6 6RD

Managing Art Editor Emily Cook
Photography Jules Selmes

Text © Alison L R Davies 2010
Illustrations and compilation
© Carroll & Brown Limited 2010

A CIP catalogue record for this book is available
from the British Library.

ISBN 978 1 904760 78 8

10987654321

Foreword by

What a strange idea: reading to your baby! It's not as if he is ready to learn to read, is it? So why bother? There are many reasons why.

Reading isn't just about working out how letters sound or how to read words. Reading is also about learning that books are great places to visit. If you read to your baby, she learns that something interesting and fun happens every time you open the pages of this strange thing. She also learns how books "work". Books nearly always work by different things happening from page to page and, if you go through the pages in the right order, there's something more satisfying that way. That's because writers and illustrators build their books towards a "gag" or a "pay-off" in much the same way as a stand-up comedian does.

Reading is also about showing your child the special value of the written language. It's easy to forget that the way we speak and the way we write are really like two different dialects, as far apart as, say, someone who speaks with a strong London accent and someone who speaks with a strong Jamaican accent. Though we forget how we did it, we had to learn how written dialect works. When we read to children, we're reading the written dialect out loud and what that does is help your child hear the "tune" of writing.

Michael Rosen

Reading is also about sharing with each other the things we think are important. Writing was invented as a way of storing ideas, feelings and facts so that books are a bit like fridges: we put in them what we might need later. Then, when we open them up, there they are! This is quite a hard idea for children to grasp. For several years, they're not absolutely sure how or why books are able to store up things. Children hear us read books to them and there is the mystery of the books sounding more or less the same. And, in fact, one of the reasons why children like the same books being read to them over and over again, is because they are learning how books can do this miracle of storing ideas, feelings and facts.

Reading is also about triangles! We know how important it is to look into a baby's eyes when we talk to him. But this is not the only way of looking. We also want our babies and very young children to discover the world in a safe way, knowing all the while that they are loved. One of the great ways of doing that is having your baby on your lap, looking out from you, but being held in a safe and loving way. Then, as you turn the pages of a book, your baby will hear your voice, while images of the world out there will appear, change and re-appear.

There is a visual education going on here, too: pictures are not reality. For example, to comprehend the world, children have to discover that while sometimes "big" and "small" in a picture represent big things and small things, at other times "big" is a near object and "small" one that is further away. That's only a tiny part of what children need to learn about pictures in order to be able to understand them.

Then, finally, I'd say this: children's books are great fun for parents. Many of them help us, as adults, understand things about our relationship with our children. Take one of the most famous: *Where the Wild Things Are*, by Maurice Sendak. Max is so naughty, he's sent to his room. By the end of the book, however, we discover that someone still loves him, no matter how naughty he is. Whatever the book does for children, I know, as a parent, that it has made me think hard and often about what to do with a naughty child. If you let them do it, books for children have plenty to say to us, too.

Contents

Introduction

Storytelling has been around since the beginning of time. It is an essential part of communication, a way to bond, to build a common landscape and to pass on information. It is also a fantastic creative tool that can be used at any age to trigger the imagination and explore language. Although it is not strictly the same as reading out loud, the two forms of telling tales are linked, and we progress from reading stories to creating tales that we want to share. So reading is the first step along the road to creativity and eventually telling and sharing tales.

This book shows you the best way to read to your baby and how to develop this skill into storytelling. It gives you information on a variety of techniques that will help fire your child's imagination and encourage a pattern of reading. Each chapter includes suggested activities that you can put into practice from day one, and I really do mean day one! It's never too early to start reading to your child.

When a baby is born only 25 percent of his brain is developed. Therefore, what happens from this point on is crucial. Getting your baby into a regular habit of reading will stimulate his senses and encourage development on many levels.

Reading is a great bonding experience for parent and child. There's nothing more comforting for a baby than that closeness that comes from sharing a story. The baby feels safe and secure and responds to the parent's voice and proximity. For parents, time spent reading together ensures they connect with their child and shut out the world. In those first few months after birth it can be difficult to actually enjoy being with your baby. Pressure and tiredness take their toll and getting through the days can seem a chore rather than a pleasure. Making sure you set time aside for a reading session is one way that you and your baby can both relax together. Treat it is as a special time, a luxury that you can enjoy, and a way of sharing your love.

Another benefit of regular story slots is that they help your child get used to books and the act of reading. Research has found that children who don't have much experience with books when they are very young, are more likely to avoid them as they get older. This is because they don't feel comfortable with books as their experience is limited. It can be hard to break patterns which are established at such an early stage in a child's development. Reading regularly, at the same time every day, will eventually get your little one into the habit of reading books. Routine is your baby's friend; your baby will feel confident and secure because she knows what is coming. This gives her a sense of achievement. She will enjoy these sessions and look forward to them. So books are soon recognised as a delight, not something to dread or be scared of.

Reading to your baby will get him used to language. Very early on, your

baby will not understand what you are saying, nor will he appreciate any pictures, but he will soon start to identify words and sentiments through the tone of your voice. Unborn babies can recognise their mother's (and often their father's) voice while in the womb. Once born, your baby knows who you are, and already has a strong connection to you. The way you use your voice, its tone and pace, can make a huge difference to his understanding. He understands a great deal just by recognising different pitches and inflections such as sensing when you're alarmed or at ease. When you read to your baby, you are also giving him the opportunity to encounter a wider range of vocabulary and to hear words that might be more unusual than ordinary conversation.

As your child develops she will gain more from each reading session. Slowly her attention span will increase. She will be able to reach out and touch a book, and make sense of the colourful

pictures. These simple things make reading more accessible and will help to stretch her imagination "muscle". Watching the range of expressions upon your face gives your little one valuable insights into the plot, and helps her recognise language. As she grows she will be able to join in and talk about a story. She will even be able to offer suggestions for ways that the story can develop. Before you know it, she will be reading the story aloud and making up her own stories to share with you. Maybe she will even act them out and engage in regular reading and performance slots.

But you have to start to read some time, and that's why starting at birth is best. Knowing how to do this and which stories to choose might seem a challenge. When is the best time to read? Do you read different stories to boys and girls? How do you make a bedtime story exciting, without over stimulating your child? How do you know if you're doing it right or that your baby is actually connecting with the tale? How can you help your baby engage with the story? All of these questions will be answered in this book, along with many more. Suggestions for types of stories will be given at each stage, and also ideas for storytelling on a larger scale with groups, at parties and with slightly older children. It's never too early to have a go at this wonderful skill and to encourage your little one to get involved.

There's no set way to use this guide. You can read the book from beginning to end, or dip into the chapters for inspiration. Share it with friends, other parents or carers but most importantly, have fun with it. Enjoy the activities and don't be afraid to try something new. If you get pleasure from reading and telling tales, then your child, however young, will do the same. If you get involved and get creative, then inevitably your child will follow your example.

1

Sharing a love of books and the written word
does not need to wait until your baby can sit
up and take notice of the world. You can start
while he is in the womb, and continue the
practice from the day he is born. What's more,
reading is good for both of you, helping you to
relax and bond and make the most of those
early months! This chapter highlights all you
need to know to get started.

Never

too soon to start

It's always been thought that a baby could hear sounds while in utero, although the belief was that they were muffled, as if hearing a noise through a vacuum. Latterly, evidence emerged that suggests babies can hear very clearly in the womb. This is because an unborn baby's inner ear is filled with fluid, which acts as a conductor of sound. So rather than

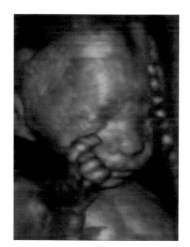

sound being distorted because the inner ear is full of air, it's quite the opposite! This interesting revelation means that babies can not only hear the inner "workings" of their mothers — their heartbeats and stomach rumblings, for example — they also can hear external noises like music, doors slamming, footsteps and voices. By the time he's born, a baby has been learning for a long while about life outside of the womb through the sounds and noises that his mother makes. It's been shown that newborns recognise and respond to their mother's voice, certain sounds and pieces of music. Thus, a baby may be soothed into sleep by songs that were played or sung to him prior to birth because he is already familiar with them and feels comfortable and reassured by their presence.

More recently, research indicates that babies can actually learn about language and speech patterns in the womb. This might sound far-fetched, but scientists have carried out a number of experiments in this area. They have collected "cry prints" of newborns, and found that they are packed with speech intonations and rhythms that match their mothers' voices and these imprints are based on the language spoken by the parents. Scientists have also discovered that babies can and do exercise the muscles they will use to develop speech while they are still in the womb.

Interestingly, the same investigations found that babies born to deaf or mute mothers either didn't cry at all, or made very strange noises. This is because they were not familiar with the sound of their mothers' voices.

This evidence clearly highlights that a mother's voice is very important to her child's development. Your baby made a connection to your voice while he was in the womb, and so the sound of your voice is key in helping him make sense of the world. When you think about this, reading aloud is not such a big leap from what you'd already been doing while carrying your unborn baby. It's the next logical step and to advance the process even more, you can start pre-birth.

Reading to your unborn baby

Set aside a regular time for reading aloud, just as
you will with your newborn. Early evening is a good
time, because it will relax you, and ideally relax your
baby in the womb so that you both get a good
night's rest. You don't have to pick children's books.
Choosing a book that you are currently reading
works just as well. Bear in mind that this activity is
about getting your baby accustomed to the pattern
and tone of your voice, so that when he is born, he
will recognise it and listen when you read aloud.

Take your time and keep your voice gentle and
soothing. It doesn't matter what the content of the
book is, the important thing is that you read it in a
calming way. You may want to hold or rub your
tummy gently as you do this, as if you are cradling
your baby.

Read for about five minutes – just
long enough so that your baby
becomes familiar with hearing a
flow of speech for this length of
time and may be soothed to sleep.
You might want to finish your
session by playing some relaxing
music. If you can, stick to the same
piece of music, as again this will
encourage familiarity. Then, when
your baby is born, you can use the
music as a sign that your reading
session is over and to trigger sleep.

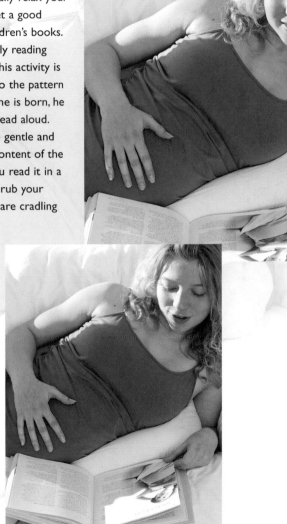

Baby's first tale

When you have a baby, from the day he is born there are lots of "firsts": the first time he smiles; the first time he laughs or says a word; the first time he takes a step; his first birthday. Every "first" is precious and essential to your child's development, but the first tale you tell your baby is probably the most important. It sets the tone of your child's relationship with reading and it's the first step on the path of self discovery and communication. It's not the tale itself, but the actual act of reading to your baby that encourages a healthy interest in language and improves literacy. We may not remember the very first story that our parents read to us, but the power and magic of books that it inspired stays with us forever!

Getting started

Soon after birth your baby will recognise your voice, so reading will be a soothing experience. Therefore, start as early as you'd like. It's never too soon to pick up a book and share it with your baby. It can also be a fulfilling way to spend the time if your baby has crying spells.

Choose a comfortable location – sitting on the sofa or propped up in bed. Hold a tiny baby in your arms, or if he's a little older, rest him on your knee so that your baby is looking up at you. Your baby may not be able to see clearly, but he will still be able to make out the shape of your face and that visual connection will help to put your little one at ease. Use body language to get your story across. This doesn't mean you have to leap

Get creative

You don't need to have a storybook to hand to have a reading session with your little one. A large, colourful picture from a book or magazine can suffice. Show your baby the picture and in a slow, gentle voice, begin to describe the image(s) on the page. What is the picture of? If it's a person, what is he or she doing. If it's an animal, what is it and what sound does it make? Make a story out of the picture. Repeat key words and keep pointing to the image(s). Repetition is vital. As your baby develops, he will start to recognise and associate sounds with images; as he becomes familiar with the elements of making up a story, he will eventually join in, and offer his own suggestions.

around the room but use your face to express the emotions of the characters. Simple gestures and expressions like a smile for joy, or a hand across the mouth for surprise, will help your baby understand and get a feel for the tale. Lean in close, and if there are pictures in the book, share them with your baby.

If your baby is older, let him reach out and touch the book as much as possible. Show him that books are to be enjoyed!

Use a soft toy

A doll, teddy or other animal can be used as a helpful character, such as "reading bear", to reinforce a sense of security. If you introduce one at an early stage, then it will become a part of the learning process. Your baby will come to associate a favourite cuddly toy with reading time and with colourful books and stories. When glimpsed, the toy will inspire a sense of comfort and expectancy to the proceedings. This will promote confidence in your little one as he develops his literacy skills.

Books to choose

As soon as you want, invest in three or four picture books to have on hand. You don't need a wealth of material at first as your baby will only be interested in the sound of your voice at this stage, not what's going on in the story. To prevent yourself becoming bored, you can alternate between the books. For the same reason, pick tales that you enjoy as you'll be reading them over and over. You might not think it's important to retain a level of enthusiasm for the tales, but your baby will notice the pitch and tone of your voice and will respond accordingly. Go for stories with interesting characters. This will allow you to use different tones of voice and facial expressions.

Most picture books contain bright and colourful images that appeal to babies. Pop-up books and those with tactile pages are even better, as they add to the reading experience. Stories with repetitive key words and sounds are a great way to hold your baby's interest, and rhyming tales work well with slightly older children. The ebb and flow of the rhyme and its pattern will fascinate them.

Painting pictures with words

Any form of storytelling is a visual medium. People often think it's about the words we use, which in effect it is, but the pictures always come first. Storytellers and writers tend to think quite visually. They build up a scene in their minds and see it as series of pictures like a storyboard, or, in some cases, a film. Their job is then to describe those pictures and transfer them to the minds of their audience, whatever its age. In essence, when we read, we've never really moved that far away from the picture books we loved as children. Reading is still about conjuring up images but we've developed our imaginations to such an extent that we can do this part ourselves, with less stimulus. In other words, when you help your newborn baby take that first step to literacy by reading to him using picture books, you're starting him on a journey of the imagination.

Building a common landscape

This activity is something you can do with small children (2–3 year olds); it's based on a simple principle of building up a picture by adding objects. Eventually you create a landscape that you can come back to again and again.

Your newborn baby might not be able to see the pictures in front of him. He can only focus on objects that are between 20–38 cms away and the rods and cones that detect colours are not fully mature. He recognises very little at such a young age, but given time, the images will emerge, and like as they do in a film, they will take on a life of their own. Using pictures is a powerful way of telling a story, and the first logical step on the reading ladder. Getting your baby acquainted with images, so that he learns to piece the story together from them, will exercise the creative part of his brain, which will, in time, help him to make connections and read words.

My garden

First get your little one to imagine that he is looking at a picture entitled My Garden. To play the game all you have to do is say "In my garden I can see…' and then add something to the picture. You can take it in turns, or if you have a larger group of children, go around in a circle, getting each child to add something new. The important thing to remember is that once something has been added it cannot be removed. Each time a turn is taken, all of the things in the "picture" must be recounted and the easy way to do this is to try and see the picture visually. Eventually, you can ask your little one to try drawing the picture, and at every reading session, you can finish by imitating this exercise and asking him how much he remembers. Not only is this great for getting small children to think visually, but it also helps them develop memory building skills. When you have done this exercise many times, the garden will become a landscape that you can explore, and a great backdrop for creating stories.

Adding animals

Ask your little one to think of the different kinds of animals that might visit the garden. Get him to have a go at making animal sounds for each one, and describing what they might look like. He could even give each animal a name and with your help create a character.

Opposite is a list of picture books with a what's in my garden? theme. Use them for inspiration and to complement this activity.

SUGGESTED BOOKS

Planting a Garden
Lois Ehlert

I Wish I Were a Butterfly
James Howe

Red Leaf, Yellow Leaf
Lois Ehlert

The Carrot Seed
Ruth Krauss

The Very Busy Spider
Eric Carle

Under a Stone **Jen Green**

The Apple Pie Tree **Zoe Hall**

Boys, girls, mums, dads

As your child gets older he will develop an interest in different types of stories. There has been much research into whether this is nature or nurture. Why do boys tend to enjoy action and adventure tales, and girls prefer magical tales with happy endings? Are we genetically programmed to develop this way? The answer is "no"; most of our likes and dislikes are formed at an early age and informed by our parents and those in our peer groups. So, the choice of story that you tell your baby is entirely up to you. The best way to avoid stereotypical imbalances is to read a general selection of tales including a mixture of different genres. As your baby grows and mixes with other children, his tastes will develop and he will naturally prefer different types of stories veering towards the choices of his peer groups. If you give him a good grounding, however, he will always be able to appreciate reading in general.

Acting out

When your baby gets a older and has started to understand the stories you tell and appreciate the pictures, why not share the reading experience. Treat the book like a short play, in which each parent takes on a role. Sit your little one between you, with the book in front, and split the dialogue between

What about mums and dads? Is one parent better suited to reading? Should each tell different tales? Again, the actual genre of the story doesn't matter as long as both you and your baby enjoy the experience. It's a good idea for both parents to take an equal share in reading activities as this will help each to bond with their baby. Neither parent is better equipped to read to a baby, and it's essential that a baby has sufficient access to and time spent with each. So draw up a reading slot rota, or if one parent works in the week and finds it hard to juggle the time, then allow him or her lots of smaller sessions at the weekend.

characters, or read short sections each. Inject expression into your voice, and your toddler will be able to distinguish the differences in the characters. This will help her form an understanding of what is going on. It's also great fun, and a wonderful family bonding exercise!

Fairy tales

Fairy tales are classic stories that have been around for centuries. Children love them, and find it easy to identify with the colourful characters. This is because they can picture them easily, and this helps them connect with the tale. The themes of good versus evil include positive messages and help little ones understand the world and some of the rules and moral codes by which we live.

Recently, fairy tales have received a bad press. There are certain schools of thought that believe these tales are old-fashioned, and that they promote stereotypes, which are unhealthy for our children. Some parents even worry that they might be too scary for their little ones, and so avoid reading them altogether.

So do they do more harm than good? In truth, the humble fairy tale, or wonder tale as they were once called, is a traditional tale that has a core moral meaning that is easy for children to understand. Fairy tales include archetypes, like kings, queens, dragons and witches, because these conjure up very specific images that little ones are able to latch onto and visualise. Not only that, but the magical themes allow children to use their imaginations, and really get lost in the story. These tales are cultural gems, and there are different versions available around the world. They're the staple of storytelling, and often the first tales we encounter as children.

Some of the stereotypes within them might seem a little old fashioned. For example, do we really want to encourage girls to wait for their prince to save the day? But the point is that fairy tales are a starting point from which we can encourage our children to read and create. As parents, we have to use common sense when it comes to reading material and some fairy tales can include scary elements. So leave these for older children and choose something light-hearted and magical for babies. Don't let them miss out these enchanting tales, even if you feel some of the topics should be updated.

Getting your child involved

As your child gets older you can try suggesting different outcomes and asking him what he thinks about the tales. How does he think it should end? Allow your child to explore the characters. Is the big bad wolf in *Red Riding Hood* really misunderstood? Perhaps there's a reason why the queen in *Snow White* is so jealous? These stories can provide an excellent springboard for older children to discuss topics, which are relevant to them. And because they have grown up with these tales and feel comfortable with them, children are able to identify with the characters and themes.

LEARNING WITH FAIRY TALES

STAGE ONE 0–6 months

Start off with a simple illustrated fairy tale like *The Three Little Pigs*. This is a lovely tale for little ones because it includes lots of repetition, and also the characters of the pigs and the wolf. Read this tale to your baby, bit by bit, and use your voice in a gentle, expressive way to repeat the phrases.

STAGE TWO 7–12 months

After a few months get your baby to point to the pictures and to hold the book. Ask him, "Where's the pig?" or "Where's the wolf?".

STAGE THREE 1–2 years

Eventually you can get your toddler involved. Encourage him to make pig and wolf sounds and to join in with some of the key phrases like "I'll huff and puff and blow your house down".

STAGE FOUR 2–4 years

Ask your child to draw the characters from the story and tell you a bit about each one. For example, where does the wolf live? What's his name? What about the pigs? Why does each pig make his house out of something different and what does that say about him? Encourage your child to have fun with this. If you have group storytelling sessions, get the children to act out the story taking it in turns to play the pigs and the wolf. This simple activity will help them identify with the characters and begin to look at things from different viewpoints.

2

How do you know your baby is enjoying the reading experience? Does she seem involved? At times it can be hard to tell. Engaging with your little one is the magical ingredient in turning your baby on to reading; it is the key to enhancing development and encouraging a love of language. This chapter tells you what you need to do and explains how to recognise the signs that signal your baby's engagement.

Engag

ng with your baby

Passing on information

It seems quite at odds to suggest you can improve the way you engage with your baby; after all, you are the parent, and you are naturally bonded to your child! But those instinctive ties can be strengthened, used to pass on information and stimulate your baby's development. Reading aloud is the perfect opportunity for you to connect with your baby in ways that normal communication does not provide. For example, research shows that looking at picture books together involves using three times more unusual words than normal conversation. So the act of reading aloud means that you are increasing your baby's range of vocabulary and allowing her the opportunity to get to grips with how different words sound. This is crucial to your baby's development, and will put her ahead on the path to literacy.

Babies learn phonemic awareness, which means to understand words and sounds in the flow of conversation, in the first eight to ten months of their lives. This skill develops at a considerable rate, so by the time a child is aged two, she can learn up to ten new words a day. That's a lot of information for a small child to take in, but you can help to hone those skills by engaging with your baby as early as possible and getting her used to the patterns of words.

The stream of speech used in reading aloud is where it all begins. It might not make sense to your baby, but it is from this flow of words that she will start to identify sounds and rhythms. Repetition is a key factor in this. The more a baby hears certain words in context, the more she comes to understand their meaning, and eventually identify them on the page.

Atmosphere and setting

To get the best from your reading aloud sessions you need to start by creating the right atmosphere. The first and most important thing is to ensure that you find a quiet spot where you won't be disturbed. Any outside noise will distract your baby and make it difficult for you both to concentrate.

You also need to make sure you are both relaxed and comfortable. So choose a comfortable chair that supports your back – one that makes it easy for you to sit upright. Hold your baby close, and position her in your arms so that you can easily see the book without craning your neck. If possible, put the book in a position that your baby also can see the pictures and your face, so having her rest in the crook of your arm is ideal. This way your baby gets used to the presence of a book, and is also able to read your expressions.

Soft lights can help create a calming atmosphere, so if you can, dim your lights but not too much or otherwise you'll hurt your eyes while trying to read.

TOP TIPS TO BOOST AMBIENCE

Consider the colours Colours can be used to activate the mind and turn a room into the perfect sanctuary for learning. Light shades work best with babies. White and cream are soothing, while pale blue stimulates learning. Lemon adds zest and is said to encourage inspiration.

Surround yourself with soft toys and cushions Cuddly toys and puppets can be used as props when you are reading, and cushions and mats can make magical spaces for little ones to extend their imaginations.

Burn some essential oil Scents stimulate the senses and have an incredible effect on our minds and bodies. Choose uplifting and relaxing oils, like rosemary and lavender. Together these scents work to leave you feeling mentally alert and calm, and will have the same effect on your little one.

Repetition and recall

The key to engaging your baby is to use lots of repetition. A baby will, over a period of time, start to recognise words that are repeated often enough. It might drive you crazy, but this is one tool that will give your child a sense of mastery and achievement. So rather than racing through an entire book, start small. Take it a page at a time, and repeat each section slowly. If your baby shows particular interest in a page or paragraph by pointing, gazing at the pictures or making noises, go through it again. When your child gets older, you can encourage her to join in by repeating the words with you. Children love the security of things that they know. That's why they enjoy hearing certain stories again and again. They know what is going to happen and they come to expect it. They feel satisfied with the way the tale concludes and the fact that they already know what is going to happen. Repetition triggers recall and helps stimulate memory building.

TOP TIPS TO PROMOTE ENGAGEMENT

Allow your baby to play If she wants to reach out, touch or even chew the book, then let her. She is still paying attention to you, and familiarising herself with the book at the same time.

Start small Read a page at a time, and over the weeks increase the amount you read to your baby.

Give your baby a soft toy to hold or chew while you are reading to her It will help her pay attention and to enjoy the experience.

Make up rhymes or have a go at singing words and phrases It might sound strange to you, but babies love sing-song sounds and anything that has a rhythm.

Repeat phrases Repetition is the way that babies learn, so don't be afraid to run through sections or words several times.

Include your baby's name in the story Although she will not understand this initially, as she develops, she will recognise her name and it will help to draw her into the tale.

Allow your baby to turn the pages with you Your baby might appear more interested in the book than what you are saying, but that doesn't matter. She is still learning about books and enjoying spending time with you.

Signs of awareness

So how do you tell if your baby is responding to a story? What signs should you look out for? Babies don't come with a manual, and each one is different. No two babies respond in the same way. You have to learn how to communicate with your little one, and read the personal signs and signals that she is connecting with you. This might sound complex, but babies are just like books. They get easier to read the more you practise. The most important thing to consider is how much attention your baby is giving you and the story. The minute she loses interest, reach for other things; if she cries, you know that she has had enough. Never try and force your baby to sit and read. Follow her lead in this and work together as a team.

Ask questions As your child gets older you can draw her into the tale by including questions. Make the story relevant by bringing it into your child's world. So, for example, if there's a cat in the story, you could say "And look there's a cat just like our cat." Point out familiarities, and then ask your little one questions, like "What sound does a cat make?" or "What would you call the cat in the story?"

Use games With toddlers and older children you can use simple story games like "peek-a-boo" or ask them where things are on the page.

Look out for

GAZE Watch where your baby is looking; if she is gazing at the book or you, then you have her attention and she is engaged.

COOS AND GURGLES You may find that your baby makes sounds while you are reading. This is a good sign because she is trying to join in. The sounds she makes will eventually develop into words, and it's her way of showing that she wants to be a part of the reading process.

GESTURES Babies often try and touch things that they are interested in. It's their way of saying "Hey, look at this, this is fun!" So look out for any movements, particularly if they're directed at the book.

LACK OF ATTENTION If your baby's gaze wavers for any length of time or she retreats from the book, stop reading. It's better to leave it at that point and come back to it another time. Bear in mind that your mission is to make reading fun and enjoyable so that your baby will always associate warm and pleasant feelings with the experience.

Stories that appeal

Make it easy to engage your child by choosing tales that are fun and colourful and provide the opportunity for lots of repetition and future story games. Here are a few suggestions for types of books.

Nursery rhymes

These are an excellent choice for babies. The rhymes are short, so they are the perfect extent for a baby's attention span. They have an ebb and

Using puppets

Invest in a hand or finger puppet that you can use during your reading slots. The puppet will help you to tell the story, and will hold your baby's attention. Point to the pages with the puppet, highlighting words and pictures and remember to include your baby by pointing and tapping her gently with it. Use it as a prop to add interest before and after storytelling. Give it a name, and a purpose – "This is Pod, Emily's reading helper". Soon Emily will understand that whenever Pod's around it's time for reading and having fun. Let your baby play with Pod and make this a part of your sessions.

flow that will appeal to tiny ears, and they are fun; you will enjoy repeating them. Using nursery rhymes regularly will help your baby retain information by learning sequences and patterns.

Cloth, bath or board books

Both practical and exciting, books made of different materials are great for little ones to get stuck into and handle. They're easy to keep clean, but the emphasis is on touching and feeling, which brings the reading experience alive.

Simple picture books

Books that have large, uncomplicated colour pictures or photographs with simple repetitive phrases are ideal for babies. Go for simple counting books or those that introduce sets of words by different themes.

Photo albums and scrap books

You don't have to buy materials especially for your baby. Photo albums are a great reading source, because they're stacked full of pictures that your baby can look at and you can describe. Also, why not try creating colourful scrap books that you can use in your reading sessions? You can put in personal pictures and photographs, cut illustrations out of magazines, or even try drawing images that will capture your little one's imagination. As your child develops, you will be able to make up stories together using these scrap books.

3

Being able to read involves a variety of skills including manipulative and motor ones as well as those involved in comprehension and conversation. In this chapter you'll learn more about these skills and the ways you can help your baby to master them.

Pre-reading skills

The necessary skills

Language skills

This is fairly obvious, but the more your baby hears language being used, the easier it will be for him to learn how to read and use that language. Your baby needs to hear his native language used in context every day. This also includes different types of speaking like everyday conversation, other children talking, reading aloud, singing, reciting poetry and storytelling. If you give your child experience of different types of communication, it will encourage him to join in.

It's also a good idea to let your child hear other adults reading, reciting and telling tales, so that he begins to understand the different styles of language, slang terms and abbreviations. Don't try and shield your child from this. Allow him to experience the full realm of expression as often as he can.

To build up your child's language skills, start a parent-and-child reading group. Get together with parents of babies roughly the same age and agree to meet up every couple of weeks for a reading session. Pool your resources and contribute a couple of books each to the pile, then take it in turns to read different stories. This way your baby will hear something

that you might not have picked for him, and he will also get used to different sounds and voices. Not only that, but spending time with other children who are at a similar level will help your baby interact and learn to play. This kind of social activity is important for small children and will help him form relationships as he grows.

Rhyming

Rhyming phrases appeal to tiny children because of their melodic flow. They sound good and are a delight to listen to, which means that your baby will pay attention to the stream of words. Research has shown that children who prefer and understand rhyming words find it easier to understand language and spell.

To help promote this skill, develop simple rhyming phrases, for example, "Peek a boo, where are you?" or "One, two, three, clap with me!" that you can use while reading and also in everyday conversation. You can add actions in with the phrases to make them even more memorable and fun. Include them in your story sessions, as an introduction, or as a game after you've finished reading.

Matching

As your child develops, he will begin to recognise patterns and shapes and later do the same thing with letters. He will match them in his mind and on paper and this type of matching will help him put letters together so he understands words.

To help promote this skill, draw squiggles and simple shapes on paper. Take your baby's finger and trace the pattern you have drawn. Make this into a fun game by introducing sounds that match the drawing. If you want to be really clever, break down letters into a series of patterns. So a W might be two rounded V shapes, or an R might be the curve at the top and then another shape for the base of the letter. You can play with letters in this way, and then put them together and trace the outline with your baby. Eventually your baby will recognise the shapes and be able to string them together in words he can read and write.

If you can, invest in foam letters that can be used in reading and play sessions. Your baby will enjoy the touch and feel of them and this will help to improve his recognition and motor skills. If you can't find a whole set, pick letters that are or will be important to your child, for example, the initial of his first name.

The mechanics of books

Babies need to learn how to look at books in the right way before they read. In other words, they need to learn basic reading skills like how you read from left to right, and how you hold a book and turn the pages. It might sound common sense to us, but we all had to start somewhere, and it can be difficult, particularly for left-handed children, to learn the correct way to read across a page.

Show your baby how to turn the page, and do this with him. Move his hand from left to right over the page, or use your own fingers to highlight the flow of words and the direction in which to read them.

Boosting pre-reading skills

There are lots of things you can do as a parent to help your baby develop the skills needs to learn to read. Here are a few ideas.

POST-IT NOTES

Leave large letters on colourful pieces of paper around the house. Try and match the letter to the object; so, for example, you could tape a big B onto your baby's bed, or a big F onto the fridge. Try and think of things that your baby sees or comes into contact with every day. Whenever he sees the object, say the letter to him, "B for Bed", for example, and repeat the phrase in a sing-song way. This is a gradual process, but eventually you will be able to develop this into a word game and leave object names as well as letters. You can even use rhyming phrases that your little one will love. So for example "B is for baby's bed, where baby lays his head!" or "B is for baby's book, where baby takes a look!".

ANIMAL NOISES

Encourage your baby to make some noise. This is easy if you have a picture book that features animals, because you can make the animal sounds. Or, if you prefer, make up your own collection of animal pictures using images from magazines and newspapers. Then play a game, by showing each picture to your baby and making the noise that goes with it. As your child gets older, you can build in some description for each animal and ask him questions like "Where do you think a bear might live?" or "What do you think he might eat for breakfast?".

SOUNDS LIKE...

When you're reading, introduce "sounds like" phrases and link them to similar sounding things. So start to spell out words by the way they sound, like "buh for boy" and then think of something else that starts with a "buh" sound like "buh for bear". Even better is to tie in your child's name, so "lee for leap" and "lee for Lisa!". Repeat these phrases every time you have the opportunity. This activity will help your baby make connections between sounds and words.

REPORT AS YOU GO

This might sound a little strange but once you get into the habit of doing this, you will notice your baby responding. Make every activity that you do an opportunity for a story. Even something mundane like washing the dishes or brushing your hair can become material that you can talk about to your baby. To make this exercise fun, you can turn it into a story by putting yourself in the picture. For example, "One day daddy decided that he was going to embark on a mission. The mission was in the very messy land of the kitchen, and his task was to clean all of the pots that had been gathering there for what seemed like forever! He started by rolling up his sleeves and filling the sink with magical soapy water...".

Listening to a constant stream of conversation is how your baby develops phonic skills, and to get used to sounds he needs to hear them as often as possible. Babies are programmed to take in an immense amount of information, but as parents we often forget and censor our communications with them. You will notice that over time your little one will start to join in, making gurgling and babbling noises. This shows that your baby is developing phonic skills and that he is already experimenting with speech.

Signs of success

There are signs and clues that will tell you if your baby is developing pre-reading skills and if your read-aloud slots and activities are working. Here are a few.

Pretending
If your baby pretends to read a book, even without actually understanding the contents this is a great sign. It shows that he knows what a book is all about, and how he should be reading even if he doesn't necessarily understand the words. Encourage this activity by leaving books around for your baby to play with.

Recognition
If your little one seems to recognise the story from the cover of the book this shows that he has started to make connections between the pictures and what the story is about. He has an appreciation of the story and how you read it. Always remember to include the cover of the book in your reading activities. Before you start, make sure your baby has seen the cover image and that you have repeated the title to him. Talk to him about the book before your read it. For example "The cover has a bear on it. I wonder if this story is about a bear?".

Vocalisation
When you're reading the book, if your baby joins in by babbling or making noises, you know that he is starting to grasp communication and appreciates what reading aloud sounds like. Acknowledge his conversation and encourage him to make as much noise as possible.

Identification
Sometimes your baby might be able to identify the difference between pictures and words. He might point to the pictures and try and vocalise what they are, or gaze at the bright colours. You might also notice that he joins in whenever you are reading the words. This kind of behaviour shows that your little one is starting to distinguish what language looks like on the page, and how it is different from images. Always talk about the pictures in

the book and point to them. Encourage your baby to touch them and as he does this, repeat what the picture is.

Connectivity

Over time your baby might start to make connections between the pictures in the book, and other objects. He will begin to understand that an image correlates to something real, and perhaps something that he encounters every day. This kind of understanding is a huge step in a baby's development. It shows that he is starting to learn what things are and how he might use them. To help, always draw his attention to these connections. Make the links for him as you are reading. So, for example, if there's a cat in the book, and you have a cat, say "And this cat, is like our cat Sally." Perhaps the sun is shining in one of the illustrations, so say "And look, the sun is shining for us, too; can you see it in the sky?" and point to it so that he makes the connection. This type of learning doesn't happen overnight, but if you repeat the process every time you read to your baby, you will notice the difference in his understanding.

Mimicking

Finally, you know that your attempts at reading aloud are working when you see your little one trying to read aloud to others. This kind of mimicking is his way of sharing the experience, of saying "Hey, this is really great, look at this!" Your child is copying what you do, and feels confident enough to share this wonderful discovery with others. Encourage your baby to play and share his books by ensuring he has regular interaction with other children. Older children are great role models, and babies will try and copy them, so get older siblings, and friends to read to your baby.

4

Why is a book at bedtime so important?
Because if you read the right story the right
way, you send your baby happily off to
dreamland and can ensure a good night's sleep
for yourself as well! Bedtime reading slots are
vital times in your baby's daily schedule and if
used correctly you and your little one can get
an awful out of it. Read on to discover the
secrets of a great bedtime read.

Bedtime reading

Stories and setting

Bedtime is made for reading. It's the perfect slot for some parent/child bonding. Let's face it, who can forget a good bedtime story? It's the kind of tale that stays with you through adulthood, and is often something you pass on to your own children. The perfect bedtime story is like a good medicine; it's sweet, engaging and leaves you feeling a lot better about things.

The perfect bedtime story has to have a strong element of satisfaction and just enough action and adventure to keep your child interested. But bear in mind there is fine line between interest and over excitement, and the bedtime story should never cross into the latter. This is dangerous territory for those who want a restful sleep! The key is to capture the imagination without over-stimulating it. You want to soothe your little one into sleep and leave her feeling that all is well with the world. Sounds like a challenge, but it's easy if you follow the advice below.

Atmosphere

Bedtime reading is as much about the atmosphere as the tale. It is as important to set the scene as it is to choose the right book (see opposite page). Bright lights and a comfortable chair may be fine for storytelling in the day, but at night your aim is to encourage a restful night's sleep. Your baby should be in her nightclothes and ready for or tucked up into bed. A soft reading light should be nearby. With a young baby, you may prefer to hold her in your lap but an older child should be in bed. Sit close by your baby's bed, or get into it with her so that she feels safe and secure. The aim here is to make your baby as comfortable and relaxed as possible, so take your time and speak to her in a soothing voice.

Always stick to a regular routine – the same time and sequence of events – dressing for bed, brushing teeth, picking a book, etc. – so that your child knows what to expect. If you start doing this when your child is a baby, she will gradually look forward to these sessions and get more involved as they develop.

Keep it simple

Many classic tales have been streamlined and made into picture book versions. These are ideal for bedtime stories as they have just enough story to hold interest, without becoming too complicated.

Time

Five to ten minutes of a story is just long enough to engage with your child, ease her into sleep, and get her into the habit of regular reading sessions. With a young baby, keep stories shorter. Aim for five minutes maximum.

SUGGESTED BOOKS

Good Night Moon
Margaret Wise Brown
This is an excellent choice for a bedtime read. It's the story of a little bunny who says goodnight to just about everything in order to avoid going to sleep. The soothing text and subject matter involves infants and encourages them to nod off

The Rainbow Fish
Marcus Pfister
A beautiful book with calming illustrations and a wonderful message; babies will be attracted to the sparkling fish scales which look even brighter at night

Snoozers: Seven Short Short Bedtime Stories for Lively Little Kids
Sandra Boynton
This is an excellent collection of bedtime tales that take about a minute to read, so perfect for tiny babies. The book includes colourful tabs so that older babies can have a go at turning the pages themselves

Hush Little Baby
Sylvia Long
Based on the classic lullaby, this book is a gentle and lovely read that will soothe your little one into sleep. The story focuses on the beauty of the natural world

The Runaway Bunny
Margaret Wise Brown
A reassuring children's story about a mother's unconditional love for her child

What to read

The stories you choose are equally as important as how you tell them. They have to include sufficient action to create genuine interest without over stimulating your child. It is also imperative that they have a satisfactory ending. A story is like a parcel: when you reach the end you need to tie everything up, so that the one being read to is happy with the conclusion and can move on. This is essential for little ones who need to be able to enjoy the tale and then drift comfortably into sleep.

Choose short stories, fables or abridged classic tales. Anything longer and you will fail to hold your baby's attention. It's important, too, not to run out of time. The worst thing you can do is leave a tale hanging. Use the five- (or ten-) minute time rule. If you think a tale is going to go over, leave it for a daytime storytelling session when your little one will be more alert.

Practise reading stories aloud to find out if they are suitable bedtime material. Take your time and use a watch to be sure you don't go over the five-(or ten-) minute boundary. Think about the words in the story, and the kinds of pictures that they conjure up. Are they magical happy images, or is there something in the tale that might alarm your baby? If you're not sure, keep the book for daytime sessions. Also think about the language you are

Adding rhythm and rhyme

Changing the sound and rhythm of your voice can instantly alter the feel of a bedtime story, and most importantly encourage sleep. It's not just about lowering the tone, you can also use lilting rhymes to help your baby drift off. Bear in mind that babies and small children enjoy listening to vocal patterns and sounds long before they can understand any words. A sing-song type rhyme is almost like a lullaby and can be incredibly comforting for a young baby. Why not try these rhyming tales to finish off your bedtime reading session?

SUGGESTED BOOKS

Room on the Broom
Julia Donaldson
A lovely rhyming read that babies will enjoy. A great tale of friendship with beautiful pictures and a happy ending

The Bear in the Cave
Michael Rosen
A wonderful bedtime read; exciting and great to read aloud, but with a nice calming ending, perfect to send little ones to sleep

We're going on a Bear Hunt
Michael Rosen
Some lovely use of rhyming and repetition. Babies and young children will love this and you will enjoy reading it

Axel Scheffler Noisy Collection
Axel Scheffler
This collection of four short rhyming tales is perfect for babies. It includes Lizzie the Lamb, Pip the Puppy, Katie the Kitten and Freddy the Frog

using. How does it sound to you? If it has a lilting sing-song quality then it is ideal for a bedtime read. If the words are short and sound sharp and clipped, this will be harder for your baby to listen to.

How you read to your child is always important, but even more so with a bedtime tale. With tiny babies you need to read slowly and gently. Use your voice to soothe and ease your baby into sleep. Linger over words that present soft, happy images, and slow the pace right down when you reach the end of the tale. With slightly older children, you can be a bit more creative, but always remember to wind down your tale by slowing the pace and lowering the pitch of your voice. You may find that your baby drifts into sleep half way through the story. If so, just let the words dwindle gently and earmark the book for next time.

Make up your own

If you're struggling to find the right tale for your baby, why not make one up. Choose a theme that is relaxing and something with which your baby can identify. So, for example, going to bed and dreaming is a great choice, because that's what you're encouraging your baby to do, and it's something she does every day. Make the story relevant by including your baby's name in it. This trick will help draw your child into the story and make her feel a part of it. With a tiny baby, the more you use her name, the more she will recognise the sound of it, and the sooner she will learn it.

Give your story some magic by introducing an enchanting character or activity. In the case of a story about going to bed, you could introduce a magic bed that takes your baby to all sorts of wonderful places while she sleeps. To make it easy for yourself, choose a different location every night. So, for your first attempt, baby could go on a journey to the Land of Nod, and you could spend a couple of minutes describing what it looks like. Think soft, fluffy landscapes to promote feelings of safety and security. Finally, give the story a happy ending – something simple like baby drifts off in the Land of Nod and when she wakes up its morning and the sun is shining, and mummy is there to give her a big hug, etc. Overleaf, you will find other story suggestons.

To add an extra dimension to your storytelling session, include soft toys or puppets, or find pictures to illustrate your tale. You could even create a special keepsake box for your bedtime stories. This is something you can add to over the months and years, and as your child grows, she, too, can add things to box that she would like to include in the stories.

You could also check out the internet. There are lots of great sites with short stories and rhymes that can be used as bedtime reads. http://www.nightnight.co.uk is a brilliant site with ideas for reading and also the facility to input your baby's details, age, name, etc. and download a personalised bedtime story created to suit your needs.

Some magical ideas

BABY GOES TO FAIRY LAND

Baby goes to where the fairies and pixies live. She plays with them until bedtime.
The sleep fairy appears and casts a spell on her by sprinkling golden sleep dust into
her eyes. Her eyelids feel so heavy until eventually she can't keep them open any
longer. She feels warm and comfortable and drifts off into dream land. When she
wakes up, she's tucked up at home in her nice cosy cot.

BABY DANCES ON THE CLOUDS

Baby's bed soars higher and higher, until she can reach out and touch the stars. They are like
dancing diamonds in the sky. As baby gets closer, she can hear them sing a wonderful lullaby
which makes her feel relaxed and happy. Baby can't wait to explore and launches herself onto a
cloud. The cloud feels so soft and fluffy and it takes baby sailing through the sky. Like a magic
carpet it brings her safely home.

BABY VISITS THE LAND OF CHOCOLATE

Baby's bed flies through a magical portal, which takes her to Chocolate and Candy World.
Everything is made out of chocolate and sweets. There are chocolate rivers and trees and
candy floss sheep with extra fluffy wool. Flowers and people are made out of jelly beans and
there are chocolate houses! Baby has lots of fun exploring and deciding which is her favourite
bit of this chocolate land. She decides to read from a chocolate book and ends up
having a nibble. The chocolate tastes so good that soon she has a full tummy and
falls asleep, only to find that she has returned home safely from her adventures.

BABY SWIMS WITH THE MERMAIDS

Baby's bed takes her on journey to the sea. It turns into a magical glass-bottomed
boat that floats and bobs on the waves. (*Take the opportunity to describe some of the different sea
creatures, the colours and the environment.*) A group of mermaids joins Baby, and carries her down
to Mer-land where she plays with the tiny mer-children, and takes a ride on a water horse.

BABY GOES TO SPACE

Baby's bed turns into a space rocket, with baby all wrapped up safely inside! Baby goes shooting through the sky at the speed of light, until he reaches space. He can look down and see the earth and all the other planets. The bed rocket takes baby to the planet Mars, where everything is red. He meets a friendly alien with three heads and a long trunk for a nose. (*You can have lots of fun with this and with a slightly older child, you can ask her to describe what the alien might look like and give it a name.*) Baby and the alien promise to stay in touch, and the alien says it will visit earth one day.

BABY VISITS TOYLAND

Baby makes a magical wish and visits Toyland, where she meets a talking bear (*just like his own teddy bear at home*). The bear shows her where he lives in the woods and they play hide and seek, and peek-a-boo! Baby plays in the doll house with the dolls, and builds her own alphabet car to transport her home.

BABY GOES TO GREENLAND AND MEETS THE ELVES

(*The perfect time to tell this tale is leading up to Christmas. It will help your little one understand the spirit of the season, and some of the well-known characters and stories.*)
    Baby's bed turns into a sleigh decorated with ribbons and bells. She flies through the sky all the way to Greenland where it's snowing. Baby plays in the snow with the elves, and watches them in their factory as they make all the toys for Santa. Baby has tea with Santa and Mrs Claus and is given a magical box as a special Christmas present. (*With babies make sure the box contains something simple, like it being filled with love. With an older child you can use this as an opportunity to get her involved in the story by asking her "What's in the box?"*)

BABY FLIES WITH THE TOOTH FAIRY

Baby hears something tapping at her window. She sees something small and sparkling and as she peers closer she recognises the tooth fairy. "Have you come for one of my teeth?" Baby asks, but the tooth fairy shakes her head and says she wants Baby to come with her on an adventure. Together they soar over all the houses, until they reach the home of another little child. The tooth fairy flies in through the window and picks up a tooth from under the girl's pillow and leaves a magic penny in its place. Tooth fairy gives Baby a magic penny and tells her that it will help her have magical dreams.

5

Stories are meant to be enjoyed and shared. The very nature of storytelling means that tales are passed on, and over time they develop and become something new. Each telling of a tale adds something to the mix, a unique quality that gives a different flavour to the story. This is why storytelling works well as a group activity. It's flexible, interactive and, most importantly, great fun! Get a group of small children together and watch the room light up as you tell a tale. See their expressions change as they go on the journey with you and watch as they interact and enjoy the experience together.

Stor

ytelling in groups

Setting the scene

Storytelling for larger groups may sound like a challenge, but if you set the scene and pick the right tale you'll be amazed at the response. Birthday parties are great opportunities – particularly to quieten over-excited guests – but you could try to instigate regular reading sessions in a fun-filled environment. You could, for example, suggest mini storytelling sessions at your mother-and-baby group or organised coffee mornings with other parents and babies in which you take it in turns to read a story. At these occasions, everyone can get involved and try reading out loud in relaxed and supportive surroundings.

As suggested in Chapter Three, it's important for your baby to experience communication at every level – including conversations between adults and other children. Not only that, but it's good for your little one to hear other people read aloud, and to get used to different styles of speech. Group storytelling is the perfect opportunity for your baby to develop pre-reading skills and also learn how to engage socially.

TOP TIPS FOR SUCCESSFUL GROUP STORYTELLING

Create a space Allocate a place for your storytelling session – a room or smaller space. A colourful rug or mat that you can put down will make the space feel special and different enough that it commands attention.

Gather the children around you Having them sit in a semi-circle in front of you means that you can see them all and they have a clear view of you whilst you're telling your tale.

Introduce a "quiet" sound Something simple like a clap of your hands or ringing a bell can mean that it's story time. The children know

that when they hear this sound, they should be quiet and get ready to listen.

Practice the five-minute rule Even the most experienced storyteller can find it hard to hold the attention of babies and very small children for any length of time. Allow five minutes for your storytelling. This might not sound like a lot, but it's the perfect amount of time, to engage with the group, and keep them interested. To keep things moving, use short, snappy tales.

Choose your story carefully If your group is mostly made up of babies, animal tales and nursery rhymes work well as the children can

How old?

Start with babies as young as you'd like. It might seem like a challenge working with a group of babies, but you are not on your own. Get the other parents to join in, and make it a bonding exercise between parent and child, as well as a group activity. This will also get your baby used to interacting with other people.

Toddlers, and in particular two and three year olds, will appreciate the benefits of group storytelling. At this age, children are becoming more aware of their surroundings. They are keen to explore and experience the world. As their perceptions widen, everything becomes an adventure, and group storytelling allows them to participate, learn and connect with each other. It will also be interesting for you to see how your child reacts and intermingles. Taking a step back and viewing this objectively, you will see how much your child has learnt, and how he is progressing.

Group size?

It doesn't matter if you're dealing with two children or ten, the same rule applies. If you have fun, they have fun. Opposite are some suggestions to make your storytelling party a real success.

join in with the sounds. For slightly older groups, pick stories with lots of action and the opportunity to use facial expressions. Choose tales that include repetition and lots of noise.

Try to maintain eye contact You can stand and move around as you tell your story, but you may find it difficult to connect with very small children if you tower above them. You need to be at their level. If you sit cross-legged on the floor, this will make the session more intimate. You'll be able to engage with your listeners effectively while still being able to use the space in front of you.

Use props if the story allows it Props can help illustrate what is happening in the tale. Soft toys and puppets work well as the children can get hands on and play with them. Depending on the age of the children, you could also get them involved in creating props for the tale.

Repetition is the key If you feel like you're losing the group's attention introduce a noise, phrase or action that the children can join in with. The secret to holding interest is to give the children plenty to take in. Work on all levels, using sound, movement and expression.

Classic tales

OLD MACDONALD HAD A FARM (0–2 YEARS)

One of the best nursery rhymes for tiny babies. You can encourage them to join in, and do animal sounds and actions. This rhyme will help them understand the different types of animals, and it's so easy to remember. Go through the rhyme once so that they become familiar with the structure, and then repeat it two or three times. It might seem boring to you, but repetition is the key to inspiring confidence in babies.

BAA BAA BLACK SHEEP (0–2 YEARS)

This a great rhyme to sing along to and babies respond to the melody. As with all nursery rhymes, repetition is the key. When you think you've done it too many times, do it once more! You'll be amazed at how much your baby enjoys the experience and you'll see a change in confidence levels every time you run through it. You can also use puppets with this nursery rhyme and actions.

LITTLE MISS MUFFET (0–2 YEARS)

This little nursery rhyme provides the opportunity for lots of actions – Miss Muffet eating her curds and whey, the spider dropping down beside, frightening Miss Muffet away, etc. It's short enough for babies to enjoy and get to grips with.

LITTLE RED RIDING HOOD (0–4 YEARS)

Another story with a big bad wolf, which allows little ones to make some noise. Repeat the phrases "What big ears/eyes/teeth you have grandma!". When you're talking in character, try changing your voice to reflect this. Make it funny, by putting on a high voice for grandma and a low one for the wolf.

THE THREE LITTLE PIGS (0–4 YEARS)

Perfect for group storytelling, this tale has just the right amount of repetition and a simple story structure that babies can latch on to. Place emphasis on such phrases as "I'll huff and I'll puff and I'll blow your house down!". You can even ask the group to join in and roar every time the wolf appears. Tiny babies might not understand the sound, but they will join in by moving, gurgling and clapping their hands.

GOLDILOCKS AND THE THREE BEARS (0–4 YEARS)

This story uses the time's three rule. In other words, three times Goldilocks attempts to sit in a chair and eat breakfast, and three times the bears ask "Who's been sitting in my chair/bed/eating my porridge?" This rhythmic style of repetition is what makes it such a hit with little ones. You can encourage the children to join in, and even act this out by splitting the group into sections for Daddy Bear, Mummy Bear and Baby Bear.

JACK AND THE BEANSTALK (2–4 YEARS)

Before you start this story, ask the children to imagine a giant. Describe what he might look like and how he might sound. Repeat the phrase "Fee fi fo fum, I smell the blood of an English man!" and encourage the group to join in by making some noise every time the giant appears. Incorporate actions into the story, for example, when Jack climbs the beanstalk, show how he might do this.

Keeping the group engaged

The key to storytelling in groups is involvement and keeping everyone engaged. If one child's attention wavers, then this will have an effect on the others. Here are some tips to help you keep the entire group engrossed.

Key words

Before you start the story, explain that there's a magic word in the tale, and that whenever you say it, you want the group to shout it back to you three times. You can have lots of fun with this by picking a silly "magic word" that the children will enjoy shouting. For example, there's a wonderful children's tale called *The King's Bogey* (see page 66). As disgusting as it sounds, children love this story, and like any good traditional tale it has a moral, which is about making the effort and having a go at things, even if you're not very good at them. So despite the funny title, it's a great choice for group storytelling. Using "bogey" as the magic word in this story adds a new dimension. It makes it funny and it also gives the group something to look out for. The children will listen intently for the magic word, so that they

can repeat it back to you. This, in turn, makes them pay attention to what you are saying, and it makes the experience fun.

You can also use entire phrases and give some kind of sign or action that the group has to look out for. For example, another popular children's story, *The Magic Umbrella* (see page 68) involves finding out what is in a special shiny gold box. So you could use the phrase "What's in the box?" and point or clap your hands whenever you want the group to repeat this phrase.

Actions

Try to pick stories that lend themselves to actions. The more actions and movements you can put into a story to illustrate what is happening, the more the group will respond and become involved. Pick simple actions like the clapping of hands, or jumping up and down. If you're working with babies, then swaying movements are great, because parents can get involved with their children and pick them up.

SUGGESTED BOOKS

The Flannel Board Storytelling Book
Judy Sierra
Has a selection of simple stories and rhymes and characters that lend themselves to puppets

The Complete Book and CD Set of Rhymes, Songs, Poems, Fingerplays and Chants
Jackie Silberg
A great selection of rhymes that you can use with small children, and ideas to inspire you

The Random House Children's Treasury: Fairy Tales, Nursery Rhymes and Nonsense Verse
Alice Mills
You can't go wrong with this treasure trove of fabulous tales, classics and great nursery rhymes, perfect for group reecitation

Knock at the Door and Other Baby Action Rhymes
Kay Choreo
This book has lots of action rhymes and bouncy games that babies will love to do together

Play Rhymes
Marc Brown
This book gives lots of ideas for rhymes and matching movements, perfect for newborn baby and toddler groups

Measure your level

This might sound obvious, but to connect with very small children you need to get down to their level. It's no use towering above them and addressing the tops of their heads. You need to draw them into the tale by making eye contact, and staying where they can see you. This doesn't mean that you can't utilise space and move around, but don't be afraid to sit and crawl on the floor. Kneeling works well because it allows you to stretch and move around, but also stay at eye level with the group. Remember that eye contact is essential. If you are reading from a book be aware that you need to put it down sometimes, or keep it on your lap to avoid it becoming a barrier to communication.

Be flexible

When dealing with groups of babies, or very young children, you need to be flexible. Allow the story to breathe and the little ones to interact in their own ways. They will make noises, gurgle and babble, and these are all signs that they are enjoying the experience and want to be involved. Don't let this distract you, but by the same token, let them take the lead as to which bits of the tale they appreciate. If they seem to be having fun while you're reading a particular section, repeat it. You don't have to stick to a rigid model of the story, just because that's how it's laid out in the book. Always respond to your audience. If the children seem to be distracted and not in the mood for the story you've picked, don't worry, move on to the next tale. If they seem interested and want to ask questions, let them. In time, you will intuitively pick up on the stories that work. You'll get to know them so well that you can move around in the tale, jumping from sections to make the experience more exciting!

Embrace your inner child

Watch a child tell a story, and you will get the event in full technicolour glory. The story becomes so important that he puts everything into it. Arms and legs fly everywhere as he prances about demonstrating what happened. He re-lives the story as he tells it, and this connection means that it comes across with energy and enthusiasm.

As adults we have forgotten this skill on purpose. We need to be sensible and practical on a daily basis, so it's hard to remember what it's like to have that sense of wonder about everything. But if you're involved in group storytelling then you need to remind yourself of those feelings and embrace your inner child. Whether you're reading or "performing" a tale, think of it from the perspective of a very young child. Exaggerate your facial expressions and movements, and get into the spirit of the tale. Practise reading a story in front of a mirror. Try to ensure you're able to make eye contact most of the time. Look for opportunities to use your expression, and amplify every movement. Remember that children, especially very young children do not understand subtlety. They cannot pick up on slight nuances or facial changes, so you need to overstate or exaggerate things and make it easier for them. Imagine you're a clown and you have to make everyone laugh. Group storytelling gives you a license to be silly!

Web Resources

Check out the following websites for more information on stories and group storytelling.

www.allkids.co.uk
A fantastic site that lists different types of stories, perfect for parents and carers of small children.

http://www.bbc.co.uk/cbeebies/stories/
The BBC Cbeebies site has a section on stories and rhymes, it also has its own games section with lots of ideas that you can use in group storytelling sessions.

http://www.mightybook.com/stories_by_kids.html
This excellent site is dedicated to stories written by children. There are read-aloud stories and simple tales that work well in groups or individually. The tales have instant appeal and are sure to hit the right spot!

http://www.fun4children.com/poems.html
This is another great story site that is written by children. There's a wealth of material available and also the opportunity to submit your own tale.

Finding suitable stories

When you're dealing with groups of children of any age, you need a story that they can join in with. The smaller they are the more repetition is required to hold their interest and give them the opportunity to get involved. Always remember the five-minute rule and, if necessary, read tales aloud before you use them to check that they're not too long, and they have the right tone and feel for the group. If you find a story is fun to read, then the children will find it fun to listen to.

Group storytelling can be a wonderful opportunity to learn about other cultures. Sharing stories arising in or about people from around the world can give your baby an understanding of other societies and how the people in them relate to each other. There's a great tradition of storytelling in other cultures and this should be explored and celebrated. It's never too early to do this.

Running a reading group

PLAN REGULAR SESSIONS

Start by forming a parent and baby group that meets on a regular basis to talk, play and share stories.

MEET FREQUENTLY

Try and meet once a week or once every two weeks to keep the momentum going. This will help you and your baby build relationships with the other members of the group. It also means that your baby will encounter different types of language and stories on a regular basis.

INCLUDE PEOPLE FROM ALL WALKS OF LIFE

A variety of backgrounds will bring colour and excitement to your sessions. Even a different language doesn't have to be a barrier to communication. Parents whose first language is not English still have wonderful stories to share, and their input is invaluable. As you get to know each other, you will begin to break down any barriers to communication.

TAKE IT IN TURNS TO SHARE STORIES

Each parent could begin by telling or reading his or her favourite children's story – perhaps one he or she remembers from childhood. Next. each parent could come up with a family story – something that may have been told to him or her as a child, or maybe something he or she experienced, which can be shared with the group. It could be about an event that their parents or grandparents related, or just a myth or folktale that is well known in the culture and which the person has always enjoyed.

GIVE FEEDBACK ABOUT THE TALES YOU SHARE

If you've enjoyed a story make sure you say so and perhaps why. As parents, it's good to talk and support each other. Encourage everyone to have a try.

EXCHANGE PARENTS AND CHILDREN

Once you have established your group, and everyone feels comfortable with each other, you can set up one-to-one story sessions with the babies in the group. Sit in a circle and pass the babies around, so that each parent gets a chance to tell a story to a different child. This is good for your baby, as once again he gets to hear a different voice and style of speech.

CREATE THEMED SESSIONS

You can tie sessions to a specific month or time of the year or make up a list of different themes and ask each parent to bring a storybook or come up with a rhyme related to that theme. Ideas include: holidays, magical lands, animals, fairies, the sea, the jungle, space, etc. Parents can either make up stories, or search for tales that match the theme. Use the internet to source new material, and in particular stories from other cultures. Do a simple word search and see what it throws up. This is a great way to source new picture books that can you use with your own baby.

REVIEW TALES AND STORIES SHARED

Have a book review slot in your group so that parents can suggest picture books that they have read with their children and enjoyed. There is nothing like a personal recommendation when it comes to finding good reading material! Test out the stories on your baby before sharing them with the rest of the group. Make sure, too, that you ask your child's opinion. Children know what they like and what will appeal to other children. If the little ones are old enough to share their views and ideas, ask them for feedback. Even if they're babies, you will be able to tell which tales they connect with and enjoy.

Storytelling games

You can use storytelling games at any level; simple "peek a boo" type activities with groups of babies, or something more advanced for toddlers and children up to 5. The games enhance the reading experience and will help to develop literacy and communication skills. Here are a few ideas that you can try.

Baby Games (0-2 year olds)

MY NAME IS...

Sit in a circle, and pretend you're playing catch with an invisible ball. Each baby (with the help of mum or dad) throws the ball to someone else; as she does this she says "my name is…" and does a little action to go with it. This might be a clap of the hands or patting the floor. Slightly older children might want to think of an action that is linked to something they enjoy doing, like drawing, eating, dancing, kicking a football, etc.

WHO IS ON THE BED?

This is a great story game for babies. Start by telling this very simple tale. "This is a story about Granny and Jack. Granny lived on a farm. Every night Granny would let another farm animal sleep in Jack's bed. Guess who's sleeping in Jack's bed tonight!
Start with a kitten and say, and the kitten said "Meow, meow, meow" all night! The next night there was another animal in Jack's bed. Guess who's sleeping in Jack's bed now?
Go through the list of animals below, and add in the animal noises. Make sure you repeat the one before until you've said the whole list.

Kitten The kitten said "meow, meow, meow" all night!
Dog The dog said "woof, woof, woof" all night!
Chicken The chicken said "cluck, cluck, cluck" all night!
Sheep The sheep said "baa, baa, baa' all night!
Pig The pig said "oink, oink, oink" all night!
Cow The cow said "moo, moo, moo" all night!
Horse The horse said "neigh, neigh, neigh" all night!

Finish by saying "And poor Jack didn't get any sleep at all, he went 'yawn, yawn, yawn' all night!". Encourage the little ones to join in, until they have gone through the entire list of all the animals sleeping in Jack's bed. This is lots of fun and they will enjoy trying to make the animal sounds.

RIDDLE AND ROCK

Babies love rhymes and this simple game will help them establish a rhythm and go with the flow of words. First learn the rhyme below:

Baby claps one, two, three,
Baby waves at you and me,
Baby rocks from side to side,
Baby shows us how to hide!

Each sentence is accompanied by an action. For the first sentence, baby has to clap; for the second, baby has to wave; for the third, baby sways or rocks; and with the final sentence, baby does a peek-a-boo action (hands over eyes).

Take each sentence and repeat it three times and then move on to the next. Once you've done this as a group, go around the circle so that each baby and parent has a go on their own.

BABY STORY ROUND

Similar to a normal story round, you're going to make up a story that includes the babies in your group. Sit the babies (and parents) in a circle, and start by saying "One day four (five, six… as many as in your group) little babies sat in a magical story circle together. There was Jack, hello Jack!" and get Jack to wave hello. "Then there was Mary, hello Mary!" Get Mary to wave hello too, and go around the group until all the babies have introduced themselves with a wave. Then go around the circle and say "Jack was very happy and he laughed," and encourage Jack to chuckle or make noise. Do the same with every baby. If they are really enjoying the tale, you can get them even more involved by introducing other actions. For example, "Jack started to clap!" Go around the group until they've all had a go, and then wind the tale down by saying "They'd had such fun in their story circle but now it was time for sleep, so Jack closed his eyes and went to sleep." Do the same for each baby in the circle until they're all calm and relaxed. This kind of impromptu storytelling is something you can do any time, anywhere and babies will love it!

Toddlers and older (2–5 year olds)

DRESS IT UP

Children love to dress up. It's fun, and it means they can use their imaginations. Create a dressing-up box that you can add to. You don't have to fill it with clothes – scarves, gloves, hats and spare pieces of material can be used in so many ways. Get the children to dip into the box and draw out a couple of items. Now ask them to put them on and make up a character. Give them a few minutes to think about this, and when they're ready get them to stand or sit on the "hot spot". Ask the children to imagine that they are under the spotlight and that you're going to interview them. Ask lots of questions about their characters – obvious ones like their names, and where they live, and also things like what they eat for breakfast. Encourage the rest of the group to ask them questions, too. Give each child a turn, and then get the children to swap clothes and do it again!

SUITCASE STORIES

Invest in an old suitcase or trunk and fill it with assorted objects. You can use a mix of everyday items, which children will have seen before, and also throw in some unusual objects. So, for example, a tea towel, bowl, fork and ball, and then maybe something like a pair of binoculars. Each child picks something from the suitcase, and then everyone has a go at describing what it is used for. Encourage the group to have fun and come up with unusual answers. So a tea towel might be used for drying pots, but it would also make a miniature magic carpet, or an interesting pirate scarf!

  You can also split the children into smaller groups and give them an object. Ask them to think of magical uses for the object and encourage them to draw a picture to illustrate this. At the end of the session you can ask each group to reveal its ideas and show its pictures.

CARD CAPERS

Tell the group that it's going to make up a story game. Give the children some small pieces of coloured card, and ask them to think of different characters that might appear in stories. Help them by suggesting a few archetypes like pirates, goblins, fairies, knights, dragons, etc. Now ask the children to draw pictures on the cards to represent each of the characters they have chosen. If they want to try writing something, let them. Finally get them to give each card they've made a number from 1 to 10. By the time they've done, each child should have a pack of ten picture cards, with numbers on them.

The object of the game is to get them thinking about the characters. Split them into pairs with their cards. First they must shuffle the cards thoroughly, and then each child of the pair takes a turn in picking a card from the top of the pack and then putting it down, a bit like playing snap. Ask each child to say something about the character as he puts the card down, so, for example, "This is a pirate called Pete and he wears an eye patch!" The card with the highest number wins, and that child collects the pairing. When all the cards are used, the child with the most pairs is the winner.

You can create a similar game with story settings. In this version, each child picks five different settings for a story, for example, the beach, the woods, a playground, fairy world, a castle. He then has to draw picture cards for each one, and gives them a number out of five. As well as playing creative snap with them, the children can use the two sets of cards together, picking cards from each pack to create story ideas.

STORY ROUND

This kind of story game works best with toddlers and small children. Sit in a circle, and explain that you are going to make up a story together. To help, you can include a story prop, for example. a pretty coloured pebble, or a piece of crystal. The story prop will move around the circle, so that each child has a turn at holding it, and adding something to the tale. Make sure that you include the story prop in the tale to make it easier, for example "This tale is about a magic crystal, and the adventures it has." Encourage each child to add a sentence or a few words to the tale. If a child is struggling, get him to say something about the story prop – what is its name, where is it from, where is it going? There is plenty of potential for ideas and the prop will help focus their thoughts.

6

If you want to find the right story for your reading sessions, it helps to know about the different styles and types available. Each one has its merits, and works on many levels, from passing on moral lessons to opening the floodgates to creativity. This chapter gives you a basic outline of the three types, and the best way to use them with your baby!

Ideas for stories

Types of stories

There are three main types of stories that you can use for reading to your baby – traditional tales, springboard tales, and memory tales. Each type has its merits. In this chapter you will find an example of each type of story that I have successfully used with groups over the years. In parenthesis I've suggested things to do to make the story go over better..

Traditional tales

This is a huge umbrella covering folk and fairy tales and also fables. Traditional tales are simple but effective. The plots are easy to understand and perfect for tiny babies. They're just the right length to hold a baby's interest, and the themes are fun and magical. Most traditional tales tend to have some kind of moral or deeper meaning, which comes across clearly. When reading to your baby, use a mixture of these tales, and also look out for modern versions. As your baby grows, you will be able to discuss the themes and ask her questions, by this stage she will already be familiar with the format of the tale and the characters.

Springboard tales

This kind of story is wonderful for slightly older children, and works well in a group environment where children can work together and come up with creative ideas. A springboard tale is a story that takes you to the point of crisis. The story is left open, so that you or your child can try thinking about what happens next. Most classic children's tales can be adapted into springboard stories. All you have to do is get to a point where the story can go in any direction, and then ask your child what she thinks should happen next. Together you can work through the tale and come up with alternative endings.

Springboard tales work well in a party situation where children can have fun together and even act out what happens next. Rather than leaving them with a blank canvas, the story gives them the first step on the ladder, by setting the scene and introducing the characters. All they have to do then is imagine what happens next!

Memory box

From when your child is baby, create a memory box to which your little ones can add. Put in your own pictures and written stories, and when your children are old enough, encourage them to share their memories (as drawings or stories) and add them to the box. The idea is that you will be able to dip into the box at any time and bring out a story that you both know and can enjoy telling together. This also provides excellent material for a group storytelling game.

Memory tales

Tales based on personal experiences work well at any age. With babies, you can take a simple memory and turn it into a fairy story. This might sound complicated, but all you need to do is include popular archetypes and a dose of magic. So the trip to the seaside when you first learned to swim might inspire a story about the day the princess jumped into an enchanted lake and the mermaids helped her to swim. When your child gets older, you can explain where the story came from and encourage her to try making up her own memory tales. Ask her to think of a happy memory – something like a favourite birthday or holiday, or maybe the day she got her pet hamster. Get her to draw a picture of this, and then ask her to share her memory with you. With a little help and direction, she will be able to turn this into a short tale that you can tell together.

TOP TIPS TO CREATE A MEMORY TALE

Choose happy or funny memories The idea is that you can tell the tale and talk about the memory afterwards.

Think in pictures Replay your memory as if you're watching a film. When you get to the crucial part of the experience, freeze frame and imagine that you have a picture in front of you. This will help you find the right language to re-tell the story.

Break the memory down You need a beginning, middle and end. Imagine there's a bridge carrying the story from the beginning to the middle and then from the middle to the end. Think of three short sentences for each section, and one word that sums up what the story is about.

Get creative Take yourself out of the story and make it about someone else. Using your breakdown of the story (see above), turn it into a fairy story with characters like kings, queens, dragons, trolls, and fairies, and add an element of magic.

Create a good start and finish Make the first sentence exciting so that it attracts attention and make sure you tie up all the loose ends satisfactorily at the end. You also want to leave the right impression, so if you're story is about friendship, then your last few sentences need to reflect this concept.

The king's bogey

Alison's traditional tale

I am unsure as to the origins of this tale, but it has been passed around in storytelling circles for many years, and it has developed and changed, as most good stories do. It's a funny story, with a moral, and it works with most age groups, although slightly older children will understand the joke at the end. Don't be put off by the title. Children respond to stories with a silly element, and this tale has some lovely language and a deeper meaning to it. This is my version of the story, with notes and suggestions that you can use when reading/telling it!

If you're in a group situation, you can add an extra element of fun by suggesting that this tale has a magic word (see *Key Words*, page 52), and that the word is "bogey". Every time you say this word in the story, the children then have to shout it back three times.

There was once a king and he was the laziest king that you could ever imagine. In fact, he was the laziest king that ever there was, for he never did a single thing for himself. He had servants to help him with everything, from combing his hair, blowing his nose, brushing his teeth, and even, dare I say it, scratching his bottom!

One morning the king was sitting up in bed. He had just been given his breakfast by the royal "breakfast giver", when a cluster of dust shot up his right nostril. He twitched and snuffled, and tried desperately hard to make the tingling sensation go away, but there was nothing he could do. The itching was so bad, that he let out an enormous sneeze.

"AAAAAAAAACHOO!" (*Emphasise the sound and get your child or children to join in.*)

When the king looked down at his finger, there on the end of it sat a big, fat, green and very ugly, bogey!

"Oh no", he cried to the royal breakfast giver, "I've just had an enormous sneeze and now I've got a big, fat, green bogey on the end of my finger. Get rid of it, get rid of it!"

The royal breakfast giver looked at the king and shook his head. He said, "Your majesty, I'm happy to help give you your breakfast, as that's what you pay me to do, but I will not get rid of bogeys from fingers". And with that the man scurried away as fast as he could. The king's face went as red as a tomato.

"This is terrible, what am I going to do?" thought the king. He stomped about his bedroom in anger, and then he had a thought. "I will get the royal nose wiper to help me!". He called for the royal nose wiper who appeared in a jiffy.

"How can I help you your majesty?" said the nose wiper.

"Well", the king sighed, "I just did an enormous sneeze and now I have a big, fat, green bogey on the end of my finger. Get rid of it, get rid of it!".

The royal nose blower looked at the king, and he looked at the

bogey on the end of his finger and he said, "I'm sorry your majesty, truly I am. But I am only employed to wipe your nose, not to get rid of bogeys from fingers." With that he fled from the bedroom leaving the king in a rage.

The king was very angry. He was so angry he felt like he had smoke billowing out of his ears! Why would nobody help him? At last, after much stomping about the room he had a thought. "The queen, the queen will surely help me!" so he called for the queen who appeared in a flurry of skirts and petticoats.

"My dear husband, what can I do to help?" said the queen (use a high-pitched voice).

The king looked almost tearful. He said in a quivering voice (which you could imitate) "Well, it's like this. I had the most enormous sneeze and now I have a big, fat, green bogey on the end of my finger. Get rid of it, get rid of it!"

The queen looked alarmed. She said, "I'm sorry, dear. As your wife I am happy to do many things for you, but I cannot and will not get rid of bogeys from fingers." And with that, she left the bedroom quickly.

By now the king was beside himself with rage. "Why would nobody help him? What was he going to do?" He stomped about the castle (you can do this, too), going from room to room and everybody he encountered he would shove his finger in their face (again, shake your finger) and shout, "Get rid of it, get rid of it!' And of course nobody would. Well, you wouldn't, would you?

The king was so upset that he thought he might cry. He could feel the tears welling up inside. Suddenly, to his surprise, a small serving boy appeared. "What's the matter?" the boy asked.

The king sighed, "Well it's like this. I had the most enormous sneeze and now I've got a big, fat, green bogey on the end of my finger, and no-one will get rid of it for me."

"I will," said the boy smiling.

"You will?" asked the king.

"Yes," said the boy. "Just follow me and do exactly what I say."

The king was so happy that he did just that. He followed the boy out into the royal courtyard towards the place where the blacksmith worked. (At this point, if you are using the story with older children you can ask them what they think a blacksmith does.)

The blacksmith had just raised his hammer high above his head, when the boy said to the king, "Just stick your finger out here."

So the king did just that. He stuck his arm out and the blacksmith brought down his hammer with a very loud thwack!

"ARGH!" cried the king. It was so painful. His finger was throbbing from where the hammer had hit. It felt like it was swelling up to an enormous size. It hurt so much he thought he was going to explode and he began to jump up and down in agony (again, you can do this). There was only one thing for it. He had to cool his finger down – and fast. He stuck the finger into his mouth and sucked hard.

"Oh that's better " cried the king, and then he looked at his finger. The bogey was gone! Suddenly he realised what he'd done. "Oh my," the king cried. "I've eaten my own bogey!" For a moment he felt shocked, and then a broad smile stretched across his face. It was the first time the king had done anything for himself, and it felt quite good. He had got rid of the bogey himself! (At this point you can ask the child or children if they can guess what the moral of the tale might be.)

Now the moral to this story is quite plain to see. Always try doing something yourself. Even if you think you can't do it, it's worth trying because it has to be better than eating your own bogeys!

The magic umbrella

Alison's springboard tale

This is a story that I use with little ones all the time. It's a very simple tale and so easy to learn and remember. It works best in a group environment. You can use the magic phrase idea by suggesting that every time you point or clap your hands the children have to shout "What's in the box?". This will hold their interest and they will become involved in the tale.

Billy liked adventures. He liked to run outside and climb the tallest trees. He liked to explore and have lots of fun and he was always up to mischief! One day Billy was coming home from school when he spotted something shiny and gold in the field.

"What's that?" he thought. "I must get a closer look."

He leapt over the fence and began to run towards it. As he got a little closer he realised the shiny gold thing was really a shiny gold box. "Wow", thought Billy, "I wonder...WHAT'S IN THE BOX?". As he got closer he could see that it was dazzling and much bigger than he'd first imagined. Again he thought..."WHAT'S IN THE BOX? It was so pretty, there had to be something special inside." The box was almost within his grasp, and he wondered if he should leave it there,

but the question was still in his mind, "WHAT'S IN THE BOX?". So he took a deep breath and opened it. (At this point you can ask the group what they think might be inside the box.)

He couldn't believe it. There, inside the box was a beautiful umbrella. (*Ask the children if they know what an umbrella is used for.*) It wasn't raining, but Billy decided to put it up and have a good look at it. As he spun it above his head he could see that it was all the colours of the rainbow. There were colourful patterns and shapes that seemed to catch the light and move. They looked like magical creatures dancing.

Billy was so busy watching the shapes move and twist that he failed to notice that the umbrella had started to lift up into the sky. Higher and higher it flew, taking Billy with it. He was dangling on the end, and could almost feel his feet touching the fluffy white clouds.

"Wow! This is brilliant!" he cried. He could see for miles and miles.

Just at this point a huge black crow swooped down and began to peck at the umbrella. (Ask the group to make pecking sounds and actions!)

"Oh please don't!" cried Billy, but it was too late. The crow had pecked an enormous hole into the umbrella. Suddenly it began to plunge down to earth. Faster and faster it went. Plummeting at such a speed that Billy couldn't look. He put his hand in front of his eyes and gritted his teeth.

But, to his surprise, instead of landing with a crash, he landed with a gentle thump, and he was all in one piece. Everything was ok!

Slowly Billy opened his eyes and looked around. "Wow!" he cried, "I don't believe it…"

Billy had landed right in the middle of…"
This is where you leave the story and ask the children where they think Billy has landed and what might have happen next. Let them come up with suggestions and encourage them to use their imaginations. You might even want to ask them to draw a picture of where they think Billy is. Give them some time to do this, and then ask them to share their ideas. Remember to ask lots of questions and encourage them to use different types of language.

The princess and the bee

Alison's memory tale

This tale is based on a memory from when I was a child and I went away on holiday with my mum and dad. It's something I've always remembered and it was easy to turn into a fairy story that I could tell. I often use it when visiting nurseries and schools, and it's great for stimulating conversation about bee's and creepy crawlies and why they are so important.

There was once a little princess, and she was the most timid little princess that you could ever imagine. She was nervous and shy, and scared of her own shadow!

The king and queen were very worried about their daughter because she was so quiet. They tried everything they could to help her feel more confident. They consulted with some of the great magicians in the kingdom. They asked the fairies to help and they even went to see the witch who lived over the valley, but no one could make the princess get over her fears. One day they heard about a great event in a neighbouring kingdom. It was to be a huge party, and all the children were invited.

"That sounds like fun", said the king, "I wonder if we should take the princess. Maybe she will play with the other children, and that will make her feel a lot better."

The queen agreed, and so that night they packed up their belongings and whisked the princess away in their royal chariot. They reached the neighbouring kingdom by nightfall the following day. By this time the party was in full swing. There were lots of people gathered in the grand hall. Dancers swirled about the dance floor, clowns did somersaults and juggled. The room was alive with activity and children laughing.

The little princess stood at the back watching. She felt more scared and lonely than she had ever felt before. Slowly she walked through the crowds of people, the skirts of the dancers swished about her and the music seemed to get louder. She could see a huge arched window at the far end of the hall and suddenly felt the urge to look out of it. As she got closer she realised that there was a big fat bumblebee sitting on the window ledge. (*You can pause here and ask your child/children what they think a bee might look like. If they're old enough they might know what a bee does, but if not, take the time to explain to them.*)

It wasn't like any bee she'd ever seen before. It was large and furry, and its golden stripes sparkled.

There was something truly magical about it.

The princess smiled. "You're a pretty looking bee", she said.

The bee also smiled "Thank you, you're a pretty little girl. Why aren't you playing with the other children?"

"I feel scared", the princess said. "I'm afraid of what they will think of me."

The bee buzzed a little and then he said "Don't be afraid. You should never be afraid of anything."

"I can't help it," said the princess. "I just feel scared all the time."

The bee smiled, as much as bee's can smile, and said "Why don't you come a little closer. Stroke me. I feel lonely and scared, too. Most of the time children avoid me. They scream when they see me."

"They do?"

"Yes,", sighed the bee. "I don't know why they don't like me."

"I don't either", said the princess. "I think you're a very fine bee!"

"That's because you're a very fine little girl!" said the bee.

Now the princess knew that bees could sting, especially if you touched them. She'd learned about it in school. But there was something different about this bee. He was so nice and friendly. She could tell that he was lonely just like her and needed some comfort.

"Don't be afraid", the bee urged.

"I'm not", she chuckled and stretched out her hand. Her fingers danced over the bee's furry back. He was so soft and warm. He felt exactly like a small teddy bear.

Suddenly a strange tingling sensation shot up the princess's arm. It was like a bolt of light stretching in every direction.

"Oh what was that?" she gasped. But rather than being afraid she felt excited. Something was happening and it was something good. She felt alive and full of light and happiness.

The king, who had been watching his daughter carefully from the other end of the room, cried out. He could see what had happened and he thought the princess was hurt. He ran towards her with his arms outstretched.

"My darling daughter, what has happened? Are you all right?"

The princess looked up at him and smiled, "Don't worry daddy I feel fine. In fact" she said her eyes sparkling, "I feel better than fine. I feel alive and full of magic!"

"You do?" The king was puzzled. He knew that bees could sting, but he didn't realise that this had been a magic bee.

"I don't feel scared any more", said the princess grinning. She turned to thank the bee for his help, but when she looked at the window ledge he had disappeared.

"I wonder where he has gone", she sighed. "But I will always remember how this little bee helped me."

And with that, she ran towards a group of children playing and began to join in. From that day onwards the little princess was never afraid of anything ever again. Not only that, but the land was full of honey, because every bee remembered the kindness of one little girl and how she'd befriended a lonely bee." (*With slightly older children you can ask them what they think the moral of the tale is.*)

Tailored tales

As your child gets older and begins to understand language and pictures he will really start to enjoy the benefits of reading and storytelling. Make your reading sessions extra special and introduce an element of magic to a story by tailoring it to your child's world. While it is possible to buy a printed product (see box), it is easy to make up your own personalised story books.

Home-grown story

Take a well-known classic tale and write or photocopy it, but leave blanks for the characters. You are going to insert your child's name into the story as the hero or heroine. Because your child will be the centre of the story, you need to pick a tale that will fit. So the main character should be a child of similar age. He or she should also be "good". If the story permits, use the names of your child's friends as well as mummy and daddy and grandparents. Even though the story is based on a familiar tale that you may have read before, you can change the name to make it unique. If you feel confident enough, you can introduce elements to the story to make it your own. So, for example, Sleeping Beauty (*your daughter*) might be lost in a dream world in which she has her own adventure. The prince could be daddy or mummy, coming to save her and giving her a big kiss.

Start by telling your child that if he makes an extra special wish to the reading fairy, then she will create a story just for him! If your child is old enough, encourage him to come up with ideas as you read through the tale together. If you're feeling really creative, you could get some sheets of paper, write the story down, and insert pictures and photographs of your little one and his friends to make it really personal.

Sample story

This story is based on the Three Little Pigs. It is a great one to use if you have lots of names and characters to put into the tale.

There once lived three little children, one called (*your child's name*), one called (*a friend's name*) and one called (*another friend's name*). They all went to school together and had lots of fun. The teacher (*use a familiar name*) loved reading to the children, and she would always tell them that they should try their best at all times.

One day the children decided that they were each going to build a den to play in. The first child (*friend 2*) wanted to make his den quickly so he made it out of paper. The second child (*friend 1*) made his den out of straw because he didn't want to spend time on it. The third child (*your child*) made his den out of twigs tied together with string. It took him a lot of time and effort, but he knew he'd done his best. All three dens looks very fine, and the children played in them and had lots of fun. But, during the afternoon, the sun went in and the sky grew dark. Great black clouds appeared and the wind began to blow.

The first child (*friend 2*) said, "My den's the best because it's made out of pretty paper and it's looks really colourful." But as the wind began to howl, the paper den shook and with one, two, three puffs it fell to pieces. The second child (*friend 1*) said "My den's the best because it's made out of straw and it's so soft to touch." But the wind came again and this time it blew even harder and with one, two, three puffs, it blew the den to pieces. The third child (*your child*) said to his friends. "Come join me in my den, it's the best because I tried really hard, and made it out of sticks and string." The other two children joined him and they sat huddled together. The wind blew and blew, and the den began to shake, but it did not move. It stayed together and it sheltered the three friends.

Later that day when they were in the class the teacher said to them. "What have you learned today?" The children smiled and said together, "That we should always try really hard in whatever we do." The third child (*your child*) said, "And that true friends always should look out for each other."

Surf the web

There are numerous sites that are able to produce printed books or stories that contain your child's name and other details of his life such as where he lives, the names of his friends, his favourite sports and activities, etc. Some may be versions of fairy tales, i.e. *Eva, Snow White and the Seven Dwarfs* while others are original tales. Search for personalised children's story books.

7

Reading to babies and small children is a wonderful tool, and it's great to get them into a routine of doing this. If you have a busy lifestyle you might wonder how you're going to fit in a regular storytelling slot but you'll find there are opportunities during the day. You can work some creative magic, too, while you're on the move, and can encourage Granny or Grandpa to do so when they babysit.

Other storyte

ling opportunities

Travelling tales

Here's the scenario. You've just set off on your family holiday, the car is chugging along the motorway and your little ones are in the back and getting restless. Eye spy only goes so far. Very small children need something to keep them entertained, and to encourage them to relax on long journeys. What better time for a story? Naturally it's not a good idea to read a story if you're driving, but if you haven't got a willing partner to take over, then you can always resort to making up a tale together. This is great fun, and another way of increasing your child's story diet.

The beauty of storytelling on the move is that you have a constantly changing landscape and you can use that to hold your child's interest. Take advantage of every opportunity to tell a story – even a simple trip to and from your child's nursery can become a chance for creative play.

Start by bringing your child into the tale. Say something like "I'm going to tell you story about a little child called (*insert your child's name*) and how she went on an adventure in a magical flying machine."

As you go on, you will notice that the story takes on a life of its own. You can move it in any direction and stop it if your child gets tired or nods off and then restart it when she wakes up. If you make a frequent journey,

TOP TIPS FOR INTRODUCING INTEREST

Add some magic Tell your child that although she's tucked up snug in the back of the car, as the journey goes on, the car transforms into a magical flying machine that can zoom through the air and go to all sorts of enchanting places.

Window gazing If your child is old enough, ask her what she sees out of the window and incorporate that into the tale.

Get creative Turn ordinary objects into something special by suggesting that although they look normal, they're in disguise. Ask your little one to come up with ideas as to what they might be. So, for example, the tall tree at the side of the road is really an old man who can change shape, and when the branches sway it's really his way of giving a wave!

telling the story will become part of the trip and your child will want to join in as she grows in confidence.

The beauty of creating a story on the move is that you have the potential to use different vocabulary. If you read the same books to your child then you are only exposing her to a limited range of words, but when you make up stories and use your surroundings for inspiration, you have so much more to work with. One example of this is cloud gazing. The sky offers enormous opportunities for inspiring stories and, in particular, the clouds, with their shape-changing abilities are able to stimulate for the imagination. If you do tell the Cloud Story (see overleaf), you can point out to your baby differently shaped clouds and say what you think they might look like or, if your child is a little older, you can ask her to do this. Encourage your child and give her ideas, and when she comes up with something, be sure to tell her that you saw a little bit of cloud dust land on her head. Although your child cannot see or feel it, you saw it land so when she goes to sleep, she'll have magical dreams. You can remind her of this gentle suggestion at bedtime to encourage a restful sleep.

Overleaf you will find some other storytelling games. If you're taking more than one child on a journey then play the red car, yellow car game.

CLOUD WORLD

There was once a world set so far up in the sky that it was made of clouds. Each cloud was soft and fluffy and smelt sugary sweet like candy floss. The other good thing about cloud world was that each cloud was different and could change shape. This meant that the children on cloud world had lots of fun. They would hop from cloud to cloud and watch as each changed shape. Sometimes they would race each other through the sky, as if they were riding flaming chariots. Other times they were happy to just sit cushioned by the softness, feeling warm and happy as they floated upwards. Cloud world was a very magical place to be, and the children really wanted to share this with the children on earth. So they decided to make a rule, if any children on earth could guess the correct shape of the cloud, then a bit of cloud dust would fall on to their heads. Therefore, when they slept, they would be able to visit cloud world and enjoy flying through the sky and having lots of adventures…

RED CAR, YELLOW CAR

Each child picks a coloured car that will be in the story. Whenever a child sees a car of his or her colour, the child has to shout out and then add something about the car's character; for example, red car likes to eat tomatoes or red car's best friend is yellow car. Soon you'll have lots of information about each car and then you can have a go at making up a story. The story should appeal to the children in your group because they have been involved in developing the characters. You can even try inserting incorrect information, i.e. red car likes to eat broccoli, and see whether the group is paying attention by correcting you. This kind of ongoing game can be used again and again, and if you've got a group of children that meet up regularly you can ask them to draw pictures of the car characters to go with the tale.

SING-A-LONG STORY

Make up words to your baby's favourite tunes as you drive along. It's fun and easy to do, and it's something your little one can join in with. With babies, try singing along a nursery rhyme to a popular tune. They will enjoy the variance of melody and the way the language flows and it will help them to relax.

Reading with granny

Remember that reading to your baby is something anyone can do. It's a pleasure that can be shared amongst family members and in particular grandparents, who will want to develop a special bond with their grandchildren. This is particularly true for those grandparents who might have mobility problems and can't be as active as they would otherwise like to be. Schedule story slots with grandparents or other family members every week, so that they can be involved in your baby's development; this will be beneficial for you and your baby. It means that you don't have to worry about fitting in reading time everyday if you have a busy job, and it means that your baby gets to hear a different voice and approach to storytelling. Not only that, but the social aspect of sharing stories is an important part of family history. It will help your child get a sense of who she is and where she comes from.

With newborns and babies

Bring with you or make sure the grandparents have a supply of simple picture books; to make baby feel comfortable, choose books that you have already read to her. Although she will not understand the story, she will still pick up a general feel for the book and the pattern of the words.

Mention to grandmum and dad that your child is not as familiar with their voices as yours, and is just starting to make associations with sound. Remind them to keep their voices soft and gentle, and to read slowly, pronouncing each word.

Show them how to hold baby close, and in a position that she can see the book and their faces so that she becomes used to their expressions.

With toddlers and older children

By now, the grandparents have already developed a bond with their grandchild and she is starting to understand a little more about the stories they tell. Refer granny and granddad to Chapter Two of the book so they can see what techniques to use to engage your child. You also should

What Grandmas do best; What grandpas do best
Laura Numeroff
Simple repetitive text and lots of fun activities, this book is the perfect read for grandparents wanting to bond with their grandchildren

Granny's Guide to Fun and Fabulous Stories
Beth La Mie
Check the website of the author and personal historian: www.bethlamie.com for details about her wonderful book Well worth a read

suggest they make up stories based on their own experiences. By creating stories based on their childhoods, they will be able to introduce a different slant to the family history.

Encourage the grandparents to create a special story place. They should find a suitable space in their homes and dedicate it to storytelling. The space should be furnished with soft toys, cushions and a story mat that they and your child can sit on together. They might even want to fill one wall with pictures to use in tales, and then add to them as their grandchild starts drawing.

They may want to have a special story bear, bunny or doll and to use it when reading a story or as the basis for a series of granny/granddad adventures that include the story bear, bunny or doll.

Story times, however, do not have to be static. Storytelling can be part of the experience on days out. Encourage the grandparents to take your child to places that are special to them, and to make up stories about the places. If they can, they should base the stories on real experiences but introduce an element of magic into them. The following tips should help them introduce the past in a fun way.

TOP TIPS FOR SHARING EXPERIENCES

Well remembered tales Pick out some of the stories that you enjoyed as a child and introduce them to your grandchild. It's even better when you have a copy of the original book.

Old family photographs These can be used to spark off some memories. Point out the different individuals and say something about each one that the child might like to know. For example, "That's your Great Aunt Mary; she used to speak in a high, squeaky little voice like a mouse!" Or, "That's your Uncle Joe; he's very tall like a tree." You might want to make sounds or actions to go with each person.

Childhood memories You can turn these into stories. For example, "This is a story about granddad when he was just a little boy, and how he got stuck up an apple tree".

Old or traditional toys It's easy to create a story and impart some history with a childhood doll or old-fashioned spinning top,

Family history story tree

This is an activity that grandparents can get involved with, and it is also something that parents can develop and add to.

You will need a large notice board and lots of pins so that you can stick up story ideas and pictures. Start by drawing or tracing a tree on a large piece of paper. Make sure the trunk is long, and give the tree lots of branches. Start at the bottom and work your way up by adding descriptions or pictures of the first few stories that you read to your baby. Encourage everyone in the family to get involved, and when they read or make up a new story for baby, they can add it to the tree. As your child grows, she will be able to add pictures to go with her favourite stories, making that story thread grow and become a branch from the trunk of the tree. She will be able to add ideas and characters, and even change the story if she wants to. Grandparents can add in stories of their childhoods that they have shared, and parents can put in future story ideas. Over time, the tree will flourish, until it's an abundance of creativity and something you can tap into at any point for inspiration!

8

A story can be used not only to entertain but also to educate your child about the way the world works – socially as well as in its physical dimension. Stories, too, can be used to introduce "scary situations" such as expecting a new brother or sister, moving home or going into hospital. Sharing appropriate stories can help a young child to experience these situations in more positive ways.

Rea

ng for a purpose

Healing tales

Healing tales are stories that teach a specific lesson, or offer help and advice. Similar to fables that have a clear moral, these tales can be adapted classics or made up especially to get a particular idea or theme across. Such stories allow your baby to learn important life lessons in a comfortable and fun environment. Even very young babies will respond to these stories, and though not directly understanding the words, will appreciate the gist of the tale, and learn from that.

An example of this is a doctor who keeps a "story bag" in his surgery for consultations with small children. He pulls items out of the bag – usually medical equipment – and he then tells a story, whilst preparing the child for his examination. The act of telling the story calms the child down, and also teaches him not to be scared of the equipment.

LEARNING TO PLAY NICELY

The specific event could be when baby cries and all the other babies in the group start crying. Because they're making such a noise, and they won't stop, the Cry Baby Fairy has to come down to earth and sort them out. Cry Baby Fairy shows them that crying at each other only makes them feel upset, and that if they learned to play together and have fun, they'd feel so much better.

KEEPING TOYS NEAT AND TIDY

Because Baby leaves toys all over the place, they easily get lost. One day Baby's favourite teddy gets put in with the laundry by accident. He goes on an adventure, which takes him to the world of Washing Machine, where he grapples with the swirling seas of soapy water. Then he's whisked away by a kind fairy godmother, to a beautiful green land only to be left hanging in mid-air by some invisible magical force. Will Teddy ever escape, and how will Baby find him? Luckily, Baby sees Teddy hanging on the washing line, and points to him. Baby realises that if he'd kept teddy with his other toys he wouldn't have lost him in the first place!

If you want to use stories in this way, you need first to decide on the message that you want to get across. What is the core meaning of the tale? What is the message you want to convey?

Pick something specific; instead of creating a story about sharing toys, for example, think about a particular incident that you can highlight. What about what will happen when baby snatches teddy away from another child and teddy's arm falls off? Teddy has to go on adventure to find a new arm. He has to go through all sorts of trials to find this new arm and baby has to help him because he feels bad for what he's done. This situation could reflect something that has happened, or something that might happen, but it's a specific incident and a starting point from which your baby can learn about sharing toys, and how to behave.

NOT BEING GREEDY

What happens when Baby wants more toys than anybody else in play group? He starts to become greedy, and he isn't happy with one piece of play dough, he takes more and more, from all the other children until he has all the play dough with which to build his own giant castle. The problem is, once Baby has built his giant castle, he's stuck in the middle of it. He can't see over its walls and he can't play with any of the other children. How does he get out? Will they hear his cries? Bit by bit, each baby helps by taking back a piece of play dough, until Baby is left with one piece. He may not have it all, but now he can play nicely with the other children and have lots of fun.

LEARNING TO MAKE FRIENDS

Baby is shy and doesn't want to play with the other children. He sits on his own in a corner, whilst the other babies huddle together and share their toys. One day an invisible playmate appears to Baby and starts talking to him. Baby is nervous at first, but he soon starts to enjoy playing with his invisible friend. He sits in the corner, laughing and chuckling and the other babies notice. Soon they come over to join Baby and find out what he's doing. Baby forgets how shy he is, and starts to have fun with all the children.

SUGGESTED BOOKS

(0 – 4 years)
One Duck Stuck **Phyllis Root**
This excellent tale works on so many levels. It's great for encouraging
speech, as it includes such wonderfully sounding words like "splish"
and "splosh" and a favourite phrase of most babies "stuck in the
muck". It helps to develop auditory memory, and the rhyming text
makes it a joy to read. It's also all about problem solving. What
happens when little duck gets stuck in the muck? How does each
animal try and help to get duck free? It's a team effort, but eventually
they get there in the end. This kind of message is important for
babies and young children to understand

(2 – 4 years)
The Last Puppy **Frank Asch**
This lovely tale is perfect for engaging little ones and it has a very
important life lesson, that while you may feel you are last at most
things, there is always something you are first at. The illustrations and
the gentle tone of the text make it the perfect book to share with
young children. Use it as an opportunity to ask your child how he
thinks the last puppy feels, so that he can start to identify with the
character and appreciate the lesson within the tale

(0 – 2 years)
Have you seen my Duckling? **Nancy Tafuri**
This colourful picture book is ideal for babies and very young
readers. It's a simple story, with few words, but the repetitive nature
of the text will encourage your little one to have a go at reading. Not
only that, the book becomes a game, as the missing duckling is
hidden on each page, and baby can have fun pointing it out with you.
There's opportunity for you to talk about the other animals on the
page, and play counting games with the ducklings

(0 – 1 year)
Baby Day **Nancy Elizabeth Wallace**
This is the perfect book for newborns and older babies. It's theme is
security and love, and the opportunity that each new day brings for
babies to learn and experience something new. There are lots of
labelled words, making it easy for babies to increase their vocabulary,
and the brightly coloured pictures will attract and hold their attention

(2 – 4 years)
The Day the Babies Crawled Away **Peggy Rathmann**
This is a fascinating tale where a toddler is the hero and saves the
day. Not only is the book a good read but there are lots of
opportunities to play "spot the baby" and get your child counting the
number of babies in the picture. The illustrations are done in a
silhouette format, which helps small children use their imaginations

Bear in mind that your story is not a lecture; it's
not about saying what is right or wrong in an
overbearing way. The idea with these kinds of
tales is that you give your little one some space
to breathe and explore what might happen. This
kind of story introduces your child to decision
making, and helps him understand how his
behaviour can affect others.

In addition to the books, below, there are
some ideas for healing tales and how you might
turn them into stories on the previous pages.
With all the story suggestions, encourage your
child to think critically about what is happening
by asking questions. Steer small children in the
right direction by giving them a clue about what
they should be looking for. So, for example, in
"Not being Greedy", ask your child how he
thinks baby is going to get out of the castle he
has built. Ask him, was it a good idea for baby to
want all the play dough? Suggest that perhaps if
he had shared it, the children could have made
something together. Draw your child's attention
to the point of the story, and give him time to
think about it.

Coping with the new

It is possible to use healing tales to help small children prepare for a variety of events or situations that they may experience. Using stories in this way means that your child will be able to think through the process in a safe environment, thus making things familiar for him and taking away the fear of the unknown. For example, the birth of a new sibling is a big event in a baby's world. It is associated with a whole host of exciting and frightening changes. Repeatedly telling stories that include this scenario and putting your little one in the tales will help him identify with the changes. You will be able to allay his fears as he learns about what to expect.

There are many books available that deal with "difficult" situations but if you can't find any at your local library or only find ones that aren't suitable for your particular circumstances, then you should to create your own story. Making up a healing tale to suit your needs might sound like a challenge, but if you stick to a simple format and use the tips mentioned in previous chapters to engage with your baby, you will find that it's an easy and fun thing to do. It also means that you can continually create tales that are relevant to your child's needs and experience.

A new brother or sister

If you are about to present your baby with a new sibling, think about he might see as the positives and the negatives. Write these down and think about the underlying concerns behind your baby's fears. For example, he might be worried that a new sibling will mean he gets less attention and love or that he mightn't like the new baby or the new baby mightn't like him? These are simple fears, but they come from your child's basic need for security and fear of abandonment. Once you have highlighted this, you need to make sure that your story addresses these fears and disposes of them in a way that makes your baby feel confident and satisfied with the conclusion. You also need to emphasise the positives of the forthcoming situation, so that your little one can think them through, and relate them to what is happening in his world.

Opposite is a simple tale that introduces the idea of a new sibling, and it will prepare your child for the changes to come. With a slightly older child, you could use the story to open up discussion and get him talking about any concerns that he may have. You can also turn this type of tale into a springboard tale, so that you get to the point of crisis – in this case where the king and queen tell the princess about her new baby brother – and you can ask your child what happens next. Get him to come up with the positives and negatives, and talk through the story. For example, is it likely that the king and queen will forget the prince once his baby sister is born? As your child starts to think this through logically, he will see that this is highly unlikely given that the prince comes from a loving family. He will come to his own conclusions. It is at this point that you can draw comparisons with your family situation.

Stress the positives

Start by thinking about the situation that you want to use in your tale – a new sibling, parents' separation or divorce, moving home, going into hospital, changing school, etc. The story doesn't have to be complicated, as long as the issue is highlighted and any fears your child might have are addressed. Always make sure that the positives of the situation are highlighted and that the ending is satisfying.

Moving house or starting school

The amount of information absorbed visually by a baby or small child is remarkable. Children acclimatise to their surroundings and form attachments to things, whether they are objects, furniture, or a room at an early age. So moving house will be a big deal for a child.

Starting school is another scary thing for a small child to deal with. To overcome potential fears, include a range of different stories that deal with change into your reading slots. Often the hardest part of starting or moving school is the fear of not making any new friends and being without the comfort of parents. So make sure you address this in the tales you tell.

A story about a new sibling

Once upon a time there was a young princess (prince) called (*insert your child's name*). She was a very lucky princess, because she lived in the castle with her mum and dad, the king and queen, and she was truly loved and cherished. She had a magical life and enjoyed playing with all her toys and running around the castle grounds, but sometimes it got a bit lonely and she wished she had someone else to play with. Someone small and fun and just like her. One day she was sitting by the magic wishing well when a small, pink fairy appeared.

"What's the matter (*insert your child's name*) you look awful glum," said the fairy.

"I'm ok," said princess (*your child's name*). "I just wish I had someone else to play with."

The fairy smiled. "Well your wishes have been answered because I know a secret."

"You do?" said princess (*your child's name*).

"Oh yes. The king and queen have a very big secret and they will tell it to you soon."

With that the fairy flew away, leaving princess (*your child's name*) very puzzled indeed.

That night the king and queen came to the princess' bed chamber and they sat on the end of the bed. The king read the princess her bedtime story, and when he'd finished, they both kissed her.

"We have something to tell you," said the queen.

"Is it a magic secret?" asked the princess.

"Yes it is." The queen smiled. "You are going to have a baby brother. "A baby brother, thought princess (*your child's name*) What did that mean? Would he be pink and wrinkled? Would he cry a lot? And if there was another little baby would the king and queen have time for her? Would she be wanted at all? "

That night the pink fairy came to her in a dream. She tapped her forehead lightly with her sparkling wand. "It won't be how you think", she said. "Having a baby brother will be fun".

"You don't know that", princess (*your child's name*) sighed. "What if the king and queen don't want me any more?"

The fairy giggled. "They will always want you. They will love both you and your brother and you will love each other. Just you wait and see."

With that, the fairy sprinkled pink fairy dust on princess (*your child's name*) eyelids and she drifted off into a lovely, deep sleep.

Many days later, the baby brother arrived. He was pink and wrinkled and he did cry a bit. But he was also sweet, and when he saw his sister gazing into his cot, he would laugh and reach up to her. The little prince would grasp his sister's fingers with his tiny hand and make her feel all warm inside. Princess (*your child's name*) soon realised that having a baby brother meant she was even more loved than before, because she had someone else in her world who she could cherish and who would cherish her back. She also had someone she could play with and so little princess (*your child's name*) would never feel lonely again!

Cover the positives and negatives As with the new sibling story (see page 88), make a list of the positives and negatives and make sure you address each one in your tale.

Add magic Accentuate the adventure of a new home by introducing an element of magic. So, for example, include a magic door or carpet that could be a portal to new and exciting worlds. You could even make up a series of short adventures and, if your child is old enough, encourage her to join in and come up with her own ideas.

Use a favourite toy or character in your tale Make your child's favourite soft toy a central character in a moving story. For example, Barney Bear goes on a scouting mission to the new house or school and has an adventure and he comes back to report how brilliant it is. Or, think about introducing a well-loved character such as Donald Duck. Talk about the day his mum made him change ponds, so he had to make new duckling friends or about when Donald was a duckling and he had to go to school for the first time. Use Donald's fears and problems to address the subject with your child.

Make up stories that include your child's current playmates Try creating stories set in the future when your little one has moved home or started school. Make sure you include your child's friends as well as mummy and daddy and other family members. Such stories will help him see that he will still have the safety and security of his old friends and family, and the excitement of making new ones too!

Going into hospital

No one likes to spend time in hospital and it's even more daunting for a small child, who will feel vulnerable and confused. The best way to deal with these feelings through storytelling is to focus on the magical nature of hospitals. Use the simple story structure below for this purpose.

Baby feels poorly.

The King and Queen send her to fairy hospital.

Baby is nervous as she's never been to fairy hospital before.

She soon discovers that the hospital is magical place with lots of other babies just like her.

She makes lots of new friends.

The fairy doctors and nurses cast a magical spell and give baby a lovely healing potion to make her feel better.

Baby is soon bouncing around and is much happier.

The King and Queen throw a huge party to celebrate Baby's return and invite all of her new friends.

TOP TIPS
FOR PREPARING YOUR BABY FOR HOSPITAL

Picture story If your child is old enough you can take the scariness out of hospitals by creating a picture story set in a hospital. Ask your child to contribute something to the picture and come up with fun characters that live in the hospital. For example pixies and elves who come out at night and clean whilst entertaining the children.

Separation and divorce

Parental partings are never a straightforward subject to broach with a child, but you can make it easier for your child to understand and come to terms with one by using the following story structure:

Mummy and Daddy live with baby whom they love very much.

Mummy and Daddy want their baby to be happy, and to do this they must also be happy, because as everyone knows, happiness is spread by the magic of a smile.

Mummy and Daddy decide to find their magical smiles in different houses, which means that baby gets to have two homes and two places to feel loved and happy.

Mummy and Daddy smile more and more, and the magic spreads until baby gets a double dosage of happiness.

TOP TIPS
FOR INTRODUCING SEPARATION OR DIVORCE

Use a positive image Using the idea of a smile as the basis for your story makes it easy for your little one to understand and appreciate what the story is about and that the outcome is a happy one.

Generalise With distressing subjects like separation and divorce, it's better to make the story an objective one, rather than putting your child into the story by using his name. The idea is to first help your child get used to the idea before taking the next step and putting him into the story. So repeat the tale using characters that your child can identify with to re-affirm the positive outcome. Then make the changeover, and tell the story putting yourself and your little one into the tale.

SUGGESTED BOOKS

My New Family: A first look at Adoption
Pat Thomas
This is a great story for new parents adopting and also foster parents to read to their little ones. It emphasises how lucky and special the child is to be part of a loving family

We'll Paint the Octopus Red
Stephanie Stuve-Bodeen
A wonderful sensitive picture book that is great for those with Down's syndrome, and also their siblings

Arnie and the New Kid
Nancy Carlson
A story about a wheelchair user and his bully, and how they develop empathy; this book can be used as a starting point for discussions on disability and bullying

Badger's Parting Gifts
Susan Varley
This is a gentle story about the death of a badger with some lovely illustrations; excellent for young children

Saying Goodbye
Jim Boulden
This is more of a colouring book but it showcases experiences of death and loss in a way that young children will understand

Death

While hard for anyone to face, for a child death is probably one of the scariest things with which to come to terms. Death plays on the basic need for security and the fear of abandonment. Knowing that he will never see someone again is something that at first a small child will not appreciate, but given time, the sense of loss increases as the reality of what has happened sinks in. Incorporating simple stories about life and death into your reading schedule will help your child understand the nature of loss and the cycles of life. These tales don't have to be heavy or morbid. For example, you can use examples from nature (the seasons changing, leaves turning and then falling to the ground before the new shoots appear). You also can use tales from folklore, which are magical and easy for a child to engage with, without becoming distressed. The idea with such a meaty subject is to simplify it and remove any taboos, thus making it something your child will eventually understand as the natural order to things.

TOP TIPS FOR STORIES ABOUT DEATH

Soften traditional tales Fairy tales can be quite gruesome in the way they deal with death. Think about what happens to granny in "Little Red Riding Hood". Rather than avoiding the subject altogether, address it in gentle manner. Talk about granny and suggest that regardless of the fact that the wolf has killed her she lives on in Red Riding Hood's heart and mind. Perhaps she watches over her grandchild, so that she is always safe and happy.

Seek out folktales from around the world There are some beautiful Native American Indian stories that touch on the subject of death, giving it a positive spiritual slant. For example, in the legend of the *Quill Work Girl*, she and her seven brothers leap to their death only to become shining stars in the sky. *Anansi the Spider*, from African culture, is always up to mischief and has many close calls with death, only to be reborn stronger and brighter each time.

Use toys to illustrate the cycle of life and death. Instead of talking about people, use dolls or soft toys as examples. For instance, when Dotty the doll is born, she is loved and played with by her human playmates. Then when she is ready, she goes to Toy Heaven where she has lots of fun with all the other toys.

Happily ever after

I like to think that reading to babies is a bit like setting the scene to a good story. You're putting in place everything that babies need to progress onto the ladder of literacy, and enjoy the stories of their lives. You are helping to build atmosphere, develop characters and describe the surroundings. It is from this point that your baby can move on, and explore language and interact with the world.

Take, for example, the Three Little Pigs – a story I've mentioned a few times in this book. You can choose to be like the first little pig, and not bother reading to your baby. After all, she is only tiny and can't understand what you are saying. Not only that but you are busy with so many other things, that it's hard to find the time. So, instead, you build your "story house" out of straw. The big bad wolf comes long, and in a matter of moments he blows it down. There is nothing of substance to hold the house together; no understanding of language, no appreciation of books and pictures, and the pre-reading abilities mentioned in Chapter Three are scarce.

On the other hand, you may decide that you're going to be like the second little pig. You do want to read to your baby, but you don't see the

point in doing this from birth. You also find it hard to make this a regular slot, and you're not too sure about letting other adults and children share their stories with your child. After all, your baby is your baby! So you make your "story house" out of twigs, and for a while it stands tall. But remember, you cut a few corners and it only takes a few extra huffs and puffs from the wolf before it all comes tumbling down. Your child does have an understanding of language and books, but she still needs to widen her perception, to be exposed to different types of language and speech for her to have the strong foundation that she need to develop.

Then again, you may decide to be that third little pig and to support and encourage your baby as much as possible. You are going to start reading to her from day one. You're going to try and implement some creative exercises and expose her to a wide range of vocabulary. In this case, you're building your "story house" out of bricks. Yes, it will take much more work and effort, but it will also be enjoyable, and a bonding experience for you both. The big bad wolf may come along and try to blow your house down, but he will fail again and again, because you have put such strong foundations in place. You have given your baby all the tools she needs to enjoy language and most of all, see and experience the benefits of reading.

I hope this book has given you an insight in to the value of reading to your baby, and where to start. There's plenty of material out there, so have fun exploring. Use the exercises in the book as a starting point, and feel free to experiment, adapting as you go along. You will learn what your baby likes and responds to by noting her reactions. Treat these as a barometer during your reading sessions and you can't go wrong!

Stories can be used in so many ways, to develop language and literacy, improve communication skills and speech, teach and heal. Most importantly, reading to your baby is a way to spend precious time together and to build those bonds that will make your relationship a very special one.

Happy Reading!

Index

Acknowledgements

I'd like to thank Carroll & Brown for all the work the team have put into making my book looks fabulous. Thank you, too, to all the mums, dads, children and babies who helped with the photography.

I'd also like to thank my mum for reading to me when I was a baby, hence my love of books, and my dad for all those bedtime Rob the Robin stories!

Finally, I dedicate this book to Thomas and Violet, two gorgeous babies who are already discovering the joy of books and the magic of reading.

Picture credits

Photolibrary.com
p2, p4, p8, p10-11, p16-17, p22-23, p24, p34, p35, p38-39, p42, p46-47, p51, p52-53, p62-63, p74-75, p76, p79, p81, p84, p87, p89

Professor Stuart Cambell p12

Illustrations by Mark Buckingham

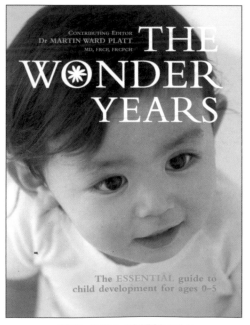